THE GARDEN OF PECULIARITIES

© 2005 Jesús Sepúlveda

A Feral House Book
ISBN: 1-932595-08-2

Feral House
P.O. Box 39910
Los Angeles, CA 90039

10 9 8 7 6 5 4 3 2 1

www.feralhouse.com
info@feralhouse.com

Design by Hedi El Kholti

THE GARDEN OF PECULIARITIES

Jesús Sepúlveda

Translation by Daniel Montero

FERAL HOUSE

ACKNOWLEDGMENTS:

The author acknowledges the important input through conversations and suggestions during the writing of this book of Kevin Donald, Paul Dresman, Liisa Korpela, Amado Láscar, Bill Rankin, Janine Sepúlveda, Wolf Sohlich, and John Zerzan. I also thank Jorje Lagos Nilsson and Álvaro Leiva for their support in publishing the first edition in the Spanish original (Ediciones del Leopardo: Buenos Aires, 2002). My gratitude also is given to Daniel Montero for translating this text into English.

1

I DEOLOGY crystallizes itself like a map in memory. It legitimizes itself by propagating the false idea that the world in which we live is the best possible world, or the system is the best system, regardless of its shortcomings. For this reason, it is common to hear that socialism is better than capitalism, the free market is better than the proletarian state, democracy better than fascism, military dictatorship better than communism, republic better than monarchy, feudal bondage better than slavery, city better than country, etc. However many of these arguments are launched, they all are ultimately absurd because they tend to justify repression at the altar of a supposed necessary order. Ideology demonizes its opposition as partisans of a supposed and constructed chaos, praising moderation and fostering resignation. Ideology skirts logic and cajoles the naive population into accepting evil as inevitable, which carries with it either the aftertaste of fatality or arrogance, but always with surrender or sacrifice. In this vein, it is not uncommon to hear it said that change is impossible, or that there are no longer ideals worth fighting for nor hope to embrace. Ideology programs collective desperation. It alienates. It defeats. It is as recalcitrant as a dogma, because its ultimate goal is self-perpetuation. It uses every means available toward this end: genocide, ecocide, elections, or simply fear—fear that paralyzes the imagination, or erases it.

Ideology operates like a narrative that domesticates by way of its own systemic standardization. It expands like a virus, or transparent and mimetic plague, which expresses itself in trends or in name-brand identities. No one sees it, no one feels it, no one touches it, yet everyone speaks with its tongue. It strangles the mind—which is connected to a server or a mainframe—and plugs in the eyes. It reproduces itself mechanically and accumulates unsatisfied desires in an oscillating spiral. This spiral is like the pleats of an accordion or, better yet, an artificial heart sounding its own agony. The beating of this false heart will continue until the empire rearms, the government regroups, castes are revived, or until the system collapses, a victim of its own decadence.

Ideology crystallizes itself like a map. This map, however, is false—it portrays the world as a mental creation, a stage constructed over the base of the gears of productivity: the gearing is the material and ideological bubble in which the so-called political and economic systems of eco-social domination exist. Ideology justifies itself with the false idea that this is a happy and viable world, and that, despite its shortcomings, it is better to close your eyes to accustom yourself to survival and to avoid any disruption of the dream. When a person dreams, the nightmares cease and fantasy flowers. This can be, however, highly subversive, because in addition to letting the imagination fly, dreams erase narratives and turn the maps upside-down, disposing of them in fetid waste-dumps.

2

DOMESTICATION is a process that some animals on this planet suffer. It reduces the wild and accustoms the animal to the absence of the natural state of living beings on this planet. It eliminates any wild characteristics that naturally negate planet-wide standardization. It erases that which is natural and spontaneous and which made life possible on this planet. It homogenizes every living creature and organizes life into unities that categorize everything living and breathing on the planet. It places human beings outside the animal kingdom, creating categories of kingdoms and organizing plants and insects as dead objects on this planet. Domestication is a process suffered like a strange sickness that weighs on life in every corner of the planet, threatening to destroy the existence of all who inhabit its magic.

3

AFFECTION instills strength. Without it, it is nearly impossible to struggle with experiences too intense and painful to endure. Tenderness is a way of life, opposed to the automatization of the clock and forced labor. Robotization is a way of death, opposed to the liberation of time and leisure, which allow tenderness to grow like a healthy trunk in the garden of all and so spread its aroma among all beings that inhabit the planetary garden. In contrast, globalization imposes a standard mold on our garden. It manifests itself in a triple process: imperial expansion of capital; worldwide standardization through economic control by transnational companies, and domestication of the soil through monoculture, destroying natural variety and paving the earth. Its avarice threatens all natural cycles. The soil is the skin and the flesh that covers our planet. Clean air is the landscape that gives us oxygen and protects us from dying, burnt by the penetration of ultraviolet rays. Condors and Magellan sheep have been blinded due to the weakening ozone layer. Water gives us life. Soil, air and water are parts of a natural cycle that pollution interrupts. Then, fire gives us the energy we need, and the sun nurtures us with compassion and tenderness.

Certainly we all need tenderness: the cat that stretches itself between the calves of guests or meows in your lap; the dog that jumps excited at your return and looks for your recognition. Tenderness reconnects us to all things and makes us well. Who has not felt pleasure at touching the face of a loved one or bathed in the pleasure of a beloved's touch?

Robotic cybernetic replicas only work. They falsely perceive time, they understand it as a continuous line where past, present and future intersect simultaneously but in an unreal way. The notion of time is an authoritarian imposition of the social order that justifies itself with the false idea of progress, a model of legitimization of the dominant order: industrialization, imprisonment and territorial delimitation. Materially, we live in the present, in existence itself.

"Hic et nunc," so goes the Latin refrain, here and now. Because of this, memory—always active and arbitrary, changing and selective— gives us a perception of our own experience. Experience amplifies peculiarity, a process distinct from history, this is to say from the standardization of the official. The only common factor to all the peculiarities there are on earth is tenderness. Affection is a primary necessity of human beings. Knowing, then is to understand that without tenderness and love, no revolution can be possible.

4

EFFICIENCY is inflexible. An automatic collector on the bus processes only exact change to print a ticket; otherwise, it does not work, and it invalidates the operation. The automatic teller buzzes at a wrong button pushed and rejects the plastic card. This is the logic of efficiency, or the reason of inflexibility. In the same way, being indecisive is a sign of inefficiency, which marks and burns with the stain of the flexible.

The sap that flows through nature spreads without a stable base of identity. Rather it flows spontaneously, precipitately. It does not reproduce itself identically, and it rejects the molds of mechanization. This fluid is in constant movement. While the river runs, its particles have no possible replica. In this way, freezing a single drop, isolating it from the general flow, is an act against nature. Cloning nature in order to pour its double into a test tube is a reifying act. Nature is peculiarity itself and is fragile like every snowflake. Its spirit is flexible. The logic of standardization articulates itself instead through the mechanisms of efficiency. An experiment cannot make itself flexible; it requires a stable pattern that must be tested under inflexible conditions and coordinates. Life flows in an organic way, like the sap of plants; it is not a laboratory experiment under scientific control. On the contrary, it flowers with the flexibility of a bud. Sap waters the world through each one of its peculiarities. Efficiency negates nature, given that it tries to impose a control panel over the garden, which sprouts spontaneously and organically. Efficiency expands and colonizes, ignoring all peculiarity. Because of this, its function is to construct categories that operate with the logic of taxonomic standardization. Thus it differentiates and creates sets while it negates the differences in these same sets, which cannot resist the light and organicity of their own peculiarities.

Reality is a garden of peculiarities forged from a constellation of other peculiarities, which at the same time disperse themselves in their own universe to the rhythm of the sap that flows and flowers. The fluid does not organize itself nor does it represent itself. It is only a flow. Everything that inhabits it is part of its own organicity, which grows in the constant movement of each unique and unrepeatable constellation. The organicity of change—which sometimes expresses itself like bubbles in boiling water—surfaces when humans concentrate their energy—which becomes self-reflexive consciousness—and corrects the course of daily events. But organicity is also natural and independent of consciousness. For example, global warming, caused by human technology, will make the planet cool down to counteract the frightening and artificial heat of fossil fuels. This will cause floods, tsunamis and even the disappearance of coastal population centers. To not understand this is to alienate oneself from the course of life that flows between each and every one of us. It is to fall into reification, that is to say, into the logic that situates subjects like dead matter in a control panel. This is the panel that turns the mechanized system on and off, negating with its measured tic-tac the permanent course of life.

5

A FEW THINGS are certain, or at least, nearly irrefutable. One of these is that life flowers around trees. Another, that trees cannot live without water. On the contrary, they dry up.

Clearcutting and the damming of rivers do not only imply the human and corporate-human dominion over nature, but also the destruction of every fountain from which life emanates. The defense of the planet, by every possible means, is not only a question of self-defense, but also of survival.

The instinct of self-preservation of the human species has brought about dominion over nature. But this very dominion threatens our self-preservation. It is a vicious circle that sooner or later will break down. And any breakdown will be a total breakdown, a rupture both mental and material because it necessarily involves our ways of perceiving and interacting with nature.

The dominion over the environment and creatures that inhabit it does not bring about preservation but colonization. Its effect is concrete: the conquest of the planet, of animals, of plants, of insects and, of course, humans. Real people, those who still have not been alienated from their own natures—by luck or resistance— still feel a strong connection with the earth and maintain a strong connection with their ancestors. Native peoples have a sense of wellbeing not seen in civilized cultures. Primitive populations still preserve an atavistic wisdom. In their eyes, the understanding that we are nothing but nature is an act of simple lucidity.

This radical revelation deconstructs all taxonomies—and epistemological classifications— that tend to justify the objectification of people in reifying categories: kingdoms, classes, races or orders of any type. Human beings are nothing but nature. Every creature is singular and unrepeatable. Colonizing cloning and the notion of a monolithic identity—as a subjective identity identical to every other identity, and thereby petrified—negates the peculiarity of every being. Civilization—and by extension its sublime expression, the city—embodies this negation. Its tendency is toward expansion, and it carries along with it colonialism and the holy war. Christian, Muslim, Inca, Aztec, Japanese, Ottoman, Greco-Latin and Chinese civiliations, among others, have shown their proclivity toward invasion and conquest. Civilization, seen as second nature, has legitimated the destruction of anything other than its own civilized order. The negation of the truly natural is the base of the civilized order, which expands like a conqueror and manifests its bloodthirsty ways in the extermination of indigenous communities and aboriginal cultures.

For civilization, every act of destruction of its icons is an iconoclastic or terrorist act. When civilization destroys a way of life or culture different from its civilized order, this becomes civilizing action. This is the logic of colonialization. The extermination of colonized communities is not just brought about by the cracking of the whip or the shot of the cannon, but also by the clearcutting of forests and the construction of dams.

6

THE INDIVIDUAL tends to see him or herself as an individual subject. This is to say, as an indivisible being, unique and monolithic. This vision has generated a false consciousness of the being that justifies pragmatic individualism as much as the Cartesian disembodiment of the self: "Cogito ergo sum," mind over body, the virtual world, personal space, etc. The institutional propaganda of school and the authoritarianism of the expert scientific voice have impelled civilized populations to internalize the notion of the monolithic subject whose incorporeal identity reifies itself into an expansive ego, thus reproducing the instrumental logic of colonizing western thought. The expansive "I" turns itself into a unique and indivisible individual, thus negating its own multiplicity, plurality and flexibility, all that constitutes its own peculiarity. Thus, while the monolithic identity negates multiplicity, disembodiment rejects reality. So, the indivisible identity reifies itself through the disembodied consciousness of the "I." And this consciousness is nurtured and forms itself through the standardizing mechanizations of taxonomic knowledge.

The individual is not a being apart from its totality, nor is it fragmented between body and consciousness. The individual is a part of its totality, and its body interacts with reality. Denying this is justifying alienation. To feel the wind, for example, that crosses our pores when we stop at night to look at the stars, is sufficient proof that this totality exists. To believe the opposite is to be sadly alienated.

Poetry and art prevent the standardization of peculiarity. Artistic language suggests, instead of describing comprehensively, the immediate presence of being. Art and poetry dismantle the reduction driven by intellectual control, allowing its practitioners to become a part of totality. This transformation is called authenticity or one's own voice, that is, the genuine that exists in everyone. This authenticity is nothing more than the peculiarity of every being: that which opposes standardization expressed by—among other things—the reification of the "I." To think, for example, that one is an image projected in a mirror, or to believe in the formal and pictorial combination of a portrait, or in a mechanically reproduced image—photography, video or film—represents an alienating distance between the reality of a being and the reifying Cartesian consciousness to which the civilized world submits. Images as mediating ideological constructs of human relationships constitute what Guy Debord early on called "The society of the spectacle." Since then, the world has conglomerated like a swarm of bees around panoptical centers of domestication: television, Hollywood, the cult of celebrity. This is without even taking into consideration surveillance and control. Images massively lead individuals to see themselves as individual subjects, that is, as indivisible beings, unique and monolithic, thus ignoring their flexibility, plurality and mulitiplicity. This final trilogy is the stuff of which the innate peculiarity of the self is made.

7

MONADS, according to the philosophic system of Leibniz, are indivisible substances of different natures that compose the universe. The neutrino, according to the physical sciences that speculate about black holes and parallel universes, is an electrically neutral particle of unappreciable mass. Human beings are part of the universe and we are all different from one another. Personality is not reproduced; it constantly grows within us. This occurs because we are divisible, multiple and flexible beings—the child who was is not the old person he or she will soon be. The obstinate personality also varies. It is unique and polydimensional. Every dimension of being is divisible by everything that constitutes it: mind, body, experience, memory, etc. To lean toward neutrality is also negating a part of the being. We irradiate positive and negative vibrations. We can also be magnetic and arbitrary.

Our bodily mass is visible, palpable, and enjoyable. It can be appreciated. The body is real. Neither the neutrino nor monads can accurately describe the human being completely. The multiplicity, which overwhelms or fulfills us, describes on a human scale, the multiplicity of the universe, the mulitude of multiple universes. Truly, everything inhabits everything, although not without contradictions. Multiple universes are a reality. It is like going to a party and meeting multiple people, parallel to themselves.

Probably, from the collision of these two universes other universes were born, grew, developed themselves, matured, grew old and died over time. At some point in this riddle we find ourselves, just like the microscopic organisms we host inside our bodies. The expansion of the universe represents its growth and aging. And it will have the right age at the moment of its dying or concentration of its multiple entirety into the empty hole. We can't do anything about this because there is no machine that can take us from this universe to another, although, of course, it is possible that death is nothing more than a voyage to other coordinates where the stampede of energy that keeps us alive is still flowing. Retaking life's path in order to correct it is what Indo-American sages believe is necessary. Maybe that would mean returning to a preneolithic stage, knowing what we already know. Is that a dilemma? There is no drama in being born, developing, maturing, growing old or maybe dying. The important thing is that in the meanwhile we can live in a state of permanent celebration. Life organized as a carnivalesque and prolonged act of being is an intelligent way of alleviating the pain. Celebrating our time on this rotating orb stimulates our community feeling. We all have to live with everyone and around everyone. We have no other choice. The state of permanent festivity leads to the joy of being and has a liberating movement. For this reason, the reveling impulse dehierarchizes and makes us happy. And in moments of tranquility, silence and leisure, it is good to appreciate the infinite expansion of the night and our growth in between the maturity of everything that inhabits the planet: the astral dome that gives us cover and lets us live.

8

B EAUTY is fragile. This is another almost irrefutable truth. The calypso orchids that grow along the paths of the temperate forest take at least nine years to reproduce. This is a heroic act of palingenesia that takes place in the middle of the forest. In the spring their rose color graces the skirts of the pine trees. But if an intruder touches its stem, the orchid eventually dies. Not so if only the petals are touched. This is the beauty of life, fragile and delicate, like everything that passes through our hands. Human beings are nothing more than nature. To pretend differently is to fall into alienation. It is to forget beauty. Usually children go to the zoo. This experience is part of our early training—it distances us from the rest of the animals. We all inhabit this planet, which feeds and gives shelter to every living thing. The balance between everything and the planet is as fragile as the orchid. Looking past the function of nature, the desire to find its utility and control it and dominate it, is a central challenge. On the other hand, to observe nature in order to appreciate it is to find plentitude. Our existence and the existence of everything else on this planet depend on this challenge. For this reason, unlearning the conditioning of our childhood in order to be able to appreciate nature's beauty is a primordial necessity.

Human beings can be beautiful creatures. But for this to happen we need to shift our perception of reality from the utilitarian to one of appreciation. In other words, we need to replace the instrumental with the aesthetic. The dominant ideological paradigm creating the present gives free rein to technological reason, but it displaces creation. Heidegger calls this latter mental agitation "poiêsis." But to replace the drive to dominate, expand and colonize—in order to radically dismantle economies based on competition and comparison—it is absolutely necessary to change the lenses through which we see reality. This is to say, refashion your perspective to appreciate day, night, the seasons, waves, the potency of rivers, the birds' songs, the movement of animals, the woods, bees, women, men and all of the constellations of peculiarities that form other constellations of peculiarities and that spring savagely like orchids in the forest.

9

THE STATE exists because it territorializes itself. It builds itself through colonizing territorial expansion. This expansion comes about through the forced deterritorialization of the original inhabitants from the lands that the state has appropriated. This appropriation implies the mobilization of military force that the state can use to expand or maintain its territory. This has meant wars and genocide. But the state also has its experts to write history; they turn the facts around so as to justify their atrocities and obligate following generations to repeat the meaningless official litanies written by the experts.

Education, then, is nothing more than the institutionalization of disciplines of training and domestication, a training ground where children and adolescents are taught to perpetuate the dominant system. There they learn to give way to the dominant order and they begin the process of reification. On these parade grounds or schools of social indocrination, the ideology that legitimates the system is reproduced. New members of society internalize a false consciousness, which inflates in them like a lung until everyone repeats with more or less success the same discourse. Its idea is that everyone says, dreams, and thinks that this is the best of all possible worlds. And if it has its faults, it doesn't matter because they can be fixed. Thinking anything different is to be part of the anarchistic ranks, to go crazy or to call to insurrection. According to Adorno, standardization obliges the subject to choose between mercantilization or schizophrenia. There is no exit from this binary mold. In this society, preferring the garden to cement is seen with distrust. And depending on the political wind of the moment, this preference can cost one's life. When the system breaks and sheep escape from the flock, prisons grow with criminal efficiency, as well as coups d'etat, raids, tear gas, repressive measures, war, etc. While all of this is occurring, the state reinforces its propaganda through radio, television and newspapers. And so the state materializes itself in the minds of individuals.

Nation states assemble their repressive apparati—police and military—to protect the transnationals and expand a lifestyle of standardization based on the reduction of humans into economic units of production and consumption. With this, a new kind of territorialization and labor slavery is produced. The technology and the goods that the global minority, dominant class uses are manufactured in sweatshops that operate with the logic of exploitation. Schools and factories are centers of control imposed by the state. In order to abolish the state, it is necessary to abolish factories and schools. The authoritarianism that the civilized order reproduces in these institutions is responsible for ethnic cleansing, political genocide, and social exploitation. In order to construct a world without hierarchies, jails, propaganda, or coups, it is necessary to sweep away the state. And it depends on us to wipe it off the face of the earth.

10

ANY ATTEMPT to standardize life is a form of domination that imposes an alienating model over people. European colonization and American transnationalization impose standardizing patterns over the differences and peculiarities of the planet and its people. Every standardizing pattern is a by-product of state and business planning, which operate in temporal-linear terms: the progression toward macrostandardizing goals that take away all liberties. Colonization fostered by the so-called civilized world negates the peculiarity of nature—people, animals, vegetation, soil, etc.—and destroys the liberty of life. To defend oneself against these perpetrations is a vital kind of will that requires thinking—with imagination and audacity—of a different world. For this reason, in the absence of educational centers it is absolutely necessary to embrace personalized education, each person teaching the other, everyone at the same time. If half of the world transfers its knowledge to the other half, there is no need for authoritarian campuses of standardization.

Institutional education reproduces in each generation the false idea that this is the best of all possible worlds, or, at least, the one that functions the best, without placing too much importance on its shortcomings. Thus, the process of normalization of knowledge through written texts—to the detriment of orality—is nothing more than the process of standardization of a certain perception of the world. In this sense, education has an ideological function: to reproduce a standardizing discourse regulated by the state. It legitimates itself through the fabricated intersection between power and knowledge, that is to say, between state control and the professional fields of experts. For this reason, the appropriation of one does not exist without the appropriation of the other. Only when groups of humans live organically in communities and cultivate their own food toward the end of enjoying the liberating pleasure of a permanent carnival state and prolonged aesthetic appreciation will formal education, as well as the exploitation of 90% of the human population and the destruction of the planet, no longer fit within the perception of reality.

The guarantor of destructive repression is the state, and it is up to us to dismantle it.

11

THE NOTION of race is linked to colonial practices. The Western World is constructed on a base of the distinction between a "we" and a "they." Or rather, between what constitutes one's own ethnicity—as if by magic, ethnicity becomes a racially neutral standardizing pattern—and "the others": that which is associated with barbarians, or the Ethnic, in modern terminology.

Ethnocentrism manifested itself in slave logic, imposing Eurocentric, supremacist categories. The Machiavellian concept of racial superiority perpetuated itself through the equating of Caucasian-European and civilized. Thus, the notion of race justified—and justifies—colonization, which is nothing more than ethnocentric dominion over nature and other ethnicities. The colonial expansion of the West classified and categorized the colonized: groups of people, animals, plants, soil, etc., through their technically self-justifying taxonomies. In this way the West marched along imposing the scientific instrumental rationality that justifies colonial practices and universal models.

Mercantile capitalism unfurled the maps and printed the dictionaries, accelerating its steamroller march. This ethnic expansion was the expansion of the colonizing ego legitimating itself in diverse historical narratives under the banner of civilization. In the name of civilization the notion of race has been constructed. This notion is the direct consequence of the instrumental mechanism of technological thinking that categorizes human experience and standardizes reality.

12

THE NOTION of humanity is tied to the notion of the world. Its origin is religious. In the West, for example, God created man and later woman. When they ate of the fruit of the tree of knowledge, an enraged God threw them out of paradise, forcing humanity to live outside of the Garden of Eden and to incessantly search for a salary and a roof for shelter. This is the justifying

narrative of domestication. Thus, God put humanity into the world. In this same way, the European
world was characterized by human presence. This
narrative was called the Sacred Word or Bible.
The sacred texts of the Middle East had other
names: the Koran, Talmud, or Torah. In these
narratives, the correspondence between humanity
and the world was built on the concept of the
chosen people: the sons of Allah or Jehova. This
religious vision is also found in some indigenous
cosmologies. For example, in the sacred Mayan-
Quiché text Popul Vuh, the creators put the "men
of corn" on earth. In this way the triumvirate of
creation, humanity and world form a discursive
triangle—ideological and religious—that explains
life through fantasies and founding myths.

These notions fell into crisis with the
European conquest. For the conquistadors, the
possibility that other human beings could exist in
unknown lands complicated their traditional
worldviews, given that it refuted their theological
doctrines of creation and that it deconstructed the
official view imposed by clergy. For the indigenous, the bearded men from across the sea were
demi-gods. Lamentably, the indigenous discovered
their invaders' true natures too late.

In this context of ideological conflict,
the idea of the New World solved the European

ideological crisis and began the long and sad cosmogonic, social and vital crisis of the indigenous peoples. Colonization starts with the notions of humanity and the world. And these same notions galvanized the push to modernity that among other things humanized nature while naturalizing control over nature.

13

COLONIZATION has been nothing more than the expansion of capital and technological thinking through the culture of standardization on a worldwide scale. This practice reached its apex with European expansion. From the beginning of the 20th century it unleashed its destructive power with the appearance of imperialism: the oligopolic phase of capitalism. This isn't, however, a phenomenon tied exclusively to nation and ethnicity building (at least not in this stage of so-called "globalization"). For the first time in recorded or remembered history a single group of individuals controls on a transnational scale a worldwide machine capable of annihilating the planet and extinguishing the life of many of its creatures, among them, human beings. This colonial stage has a monetary drive whose basis is ideological. Capital needs to standardize lifestyles, cultural values, architecture, language, landscape, thinking, etc. It looks to, in sum, make uniform the perception of reality, thus assuring its own permanent expansion. Its ideological foundation, which rationalizes conquest as an index of growth, assigns a positive value to the expansionist drive. Growth for growth's sake, invading to invade, and eternal expansion are the axes that form the rationale for expansion. They also constitute the logic of capital, which grows and spreads until it consumes and destroys all of those host organisms that allow and shelter life on the planet. Expansion is, without doubt, the ideology of cancer, which will not stop until it reaches an implacable metastasis.

14

IN THE PAMPHLET "Reform or Revolution," written at the end of the 19th century, Rosa Luxemburg advocated the end of the salary system, in opposition to the reformist program of Bernstein, which was centered in the labor struggles for better wages through systemic reforms. The history of social struggle in the last few centuries has been divided into two camps with different totalitarian tendencies: those who prefer the ends to the means or vice versa. This has led to sectarian or naive politics, in turn leading, depending on the particulars of the case, to fanaticism or vacillation. The radical course is certainly to abolish the wage system. However, faced with a situation of subsistence or material want, every penny means a substantial difference in terms of the daily survival of the dispossessed. To deny this penny to those who die of hunger every day is to fall into vanguardist self-righteousness. It is to deny solidarity.

Capitalism, whether state or private, has taken advantage of the reduction of human life to the realm of the material. By raising standards of living, it has laid waste to quality of existence, and it has destroyed on a terrible scale our natural resources. In societies that are dependent on mass production, the notion of a good standard of living functions as a counterweight to compensate for the alienation produced by the industrial way of life, and at the same time this notion creates the fantasy of consumption. To be able to choose between manufactured products—produced by forced labor in a dependence economy—is seen as an exercise of liberty. This is clearly a strategy of standardization. In the current model, the worker's role is to form part of the systemic gears that limit the possibilities of imagination and enslave human life through wage dependence. Salary is a quantification of the value that the system assigns to every human life. Its ultimate function is the mercantilization of human beings. Every individual in this process is reduced to an economic unit—or piece of merchandise—whose labor is to produce and consume. In this way the subject acts as one more input to the productive paraphernalia imposed by social machinery. Established differences between groups and classes are not only related to the position and role assigned in this paraphernalia, but also to the capacity for consumption and acquisition of goods and services. This consumerism is destined to decompress labor pressure, bureaucratic-administrative insanity, and the injustices of the process of the sale of the labor force. Two elements guarantee submission to the social system. On one hand, forced dependence of entire populations on the companies that make and distribute products of mass consumption. On the other hand, the maintenance of a high number of marginalized peoples, seasonal workers and the permanently unemployed, who operate, according to Marx, as a "reserve army." In this case, getting a job is often a privilege that permits subsistence, erasing and hiding its enslaving and domesticating character. It is reinforced by sedentarism and subjugation to a rigid schedule, symbolized by the act of "punching the clock," or the factory whistle that announces the return from lunch hour.

In the Romance languages the word work comes from the Latin root "tripalium": the name given to an instrument of torture used by the Romans which consisted of a framework of three sticks. In the Anglo-Saxon world, the word "work" comes from the Scottish "weorc," a theological term that refers to all the moral activities that can be considered justification of life. Usually its use is in contrast to the idea of "destiny" or "grace." The imposition of work as a torturous activity, or justifying action of hypocritical and self-righteous pragmatism, is a way of assuring domestication. Salaried work assures the territorialization of entire populations in zones delimited by authoritarian institutions. In this way, the state guarantees the sedentarism and social control necessary to administrate production.

The Latin "domus" means house, the etymological root of *dom*estication and *dom*iciliation —two processes, which articulate themselves together in the sense that the state extends its material presence to establish its *dom*inion. A clear example of territorialization can be found in indigenous reservations, which openly emulate concentration camps or state relocation centers.

Ghettoes are another example. There is also constant repression of those who are in permanent movement: nomads, gypsies, vagabonds, etc. In the present circumstances, dominant legality provides no space for the homeless: indigents that the system rejects and ignores because they alter the process of domiciliation. Curfew and state of siege are two crudely repressive manifestations created by this process. Certainly, along with domiciliation comes numbering. First it was numbers on houses, later individuals: telephone numbers, computer passwords, national identification numbers, social security or union cards, etc. This is how ideology constructs its methods of identification and inserts the notion of identity while at the same time fostering human commodification. Every creature is converted into a digit easily archived, categorized and reified. Domestic animals are numbered and become domestic fetishes. People are transformed into pure merchandise of numbered identity. This numeric social role is mediated by the market, through the assigning of digits that classify everyone as such and such unit of production, consumption, profit or loss. This is the true wage. And for this reason, the wage system and monetary value are inherent to the system. To undo one it is necessary to destroy the other.

The utilitarian ideology that reduces human life to the realm of the material and economic is the matrix of the system. Its theoretical base is part of the different narratives elaborated by instrumental reason. Its political practice is domestication, which is supported by the squads of state repression and the self-justifying legal body. Its objective is the perpetuation of the civilized order. This falsifies the world, promoting a perception of reality distant from true totality and reducing life to artificially constructed numbers (eg graphs and statistics.) In order to dismantle this ideology it is necessary to avoid standardizing reduction and to foment the flowering of the peculiarities of every creature that inhabits the planet.

Perhaps the first step is to learn to appreciate all that which is found outside of the civilized order, eluding the civilizing gestures so many times taught in the home and school. Maybe it is necessary to imagine an existence full of ends and means, which intersect—as Octavio Paz says—in a "perpetual present." Maybe it won't be so difficult to recognize the necessity of leisure. Maybe solidarity is possible without having to choose a, b, c or d, the base of the cretinizing logic of multiple choice. The contradiction between revolution and reform is not quite accurate; it certainly varies according to the state of the perpetual present. An individual is revolutionary only when there is revolution; the rest of the time he or she resists or provokes authority. And in neither case should solidarity retract the ends or the means. If it were this way, it would mean that everything human and natural had been reduced to the zone of the economic. It would also mean that nothing had changed, except the jargon that accelerates or slows down the rhetoric of the friction that plays along the executioner's wall during war or class struggle.

15

PATRIARCHY manifests itself clearly in daily human interaction. If a man has a strong personality, he is considered charismatic. But for a woman the system assigns the pejorative marks of bitch, dyke, or meddler. Patriarchy is a reality of oppression and control. It reaffirms itself with rape and physical violence. And it exists in the sense that the genders are separated into categories whose ideological essence lies in the presumption of certain physical characteristics: psychological, social, emotional, intellectual, moral, etc., distinguished by gender. To think, for example, that women are in general one way and men in general another presupposes the existence of profiles determined categorically by sex: men on one side, women on the other. Patriarchy is, on the one hand, a discourse written by men to justify masculine privilege and, on the other, a repressive political practice. It is ideology and power. And it depends on gender separation. Otherwise, the whole world would degenerate. In order to dismantle patriarchy, it is necessary to recreate another discourse, a discourse that will not only degenerate ideology but also establish a new form of political relationships.

Politics is a notion proceeding from the concept of "polis": the ancient Greek city, which was the germ of western civilization. Its organization is configured definitively by the Roman idea of "public thing" (from the Latin "res publicus"). In ancient Rome, public—or common— matters were in the hands of a group of patrician men. Early on they wrote the law that relegated women to another space, outside of the public space. In Greece, poets were also expelled from this public space. The Platonic project of the "Republic" did not consider either artists or poets to have sufficient merit to integrate into matters of state. Of course, women were relegated to the home. In reality, everyone except the patricians was expelled from public matters. In order to justify the expulsion of the aesthetic from public matters, Plato repeated insistently "poets were liars," given that they did not fit with his sophist logic. In the same way, they were also considered *effeminate* and *sentimental.* This is something that is still repeated and thought in various circles, especially those relating to power. The infantilization of women, poets and artists, of indigenous people, minorities, primitive cultures, etc. has been carried out through exile to the feminine sphere. This is associated pejoratively with the weak, emotional, and illogical. Said notion was early on learned via force by the colonized communities and later universalized by the civilizing *logos*: instrumental logical thought. So, the public thing (res publicus) reifies social and intersubjective interaction among humans and accelerates the process of reification.

In Spanish, to speak of "reses" (cows)—to refer to cattle—is to speak of things. For the logos, nature is a thing that is instrumentalized. Patriarchy has instrumentalized not only women, but also men. It is, to be sure, an ideological ramification of instrumental reason, because it constructs generic categories between men and women in order to suppress and control.

Peculiarity dismantles these categories. A woman is a peculiar and unrepeatable creature. A man is another peculiar and unrepeatable creature.

The categories "woman" and "man" tend to annul this peculiarity while simultaneously engendering separatism. Maybe the only possible politics that truly destroys hierarchical forms of social and intersubjective interrelation would be through the carnival. This is a festival in which all of the petals of human peculiarity unfold without systemic bases, except those ordered by nature itself. And it should be celebrated every day. All of us have a place in the planetary garden: men and women, boys and girls, the elderly. Our biological differences or sexual preferences do not have to mean that some are banished from the planetary garden. The distinction between private and public has been constructed artificially in order to guarantee the repressive functioning of patriarchical control. To abolish this distinction would also mean abolishing gender notions that marked the beginning of Western civilization.

16

THE DIVISION of labor is not in itself the notion that produced technological-instrumental thinking. It was a kind of division of labor, organized in such a way so that some began to benefit from the labor force of others. The division of labor is nothing more than a practice. In contrast, instrumental reason is the product of the practice of control which generates sophisticated forms of labor division, put in place in societies of mass production in which the standardization of the world crystallizes itself: in cities. In communities constructed on a human scale, with direct and personal social relations, face-to-face, the practices of instrumental control don't fit. What do fit are practices of mutual cooperation. For example, while someone cooks, another prepares the seed beds to cultivate garden vegetables, or works the soil of the plot, where the beds will be created. Others gather firewood or collect the fruits of the orchard. When a woman gives birth, others help with water and care. While some have more energy, others, like the elderly, walk more slowly. This is the way of life and the organic movement of nature, divided into seasons, days and nights. There is a pendular temporality. The division of labor can be an organic behavior of social activity instead of a salaried imposition that conditions life. In a community constructed on human scale it is impossible to do everything. Ubiquity has been denied us. When everyone does a little of everything, simultaneously, or in parallel rhythms, without specialization, it will be possible to live in the perpetual present. Only in this way can we transgress the linear notion of planned time. When our existence achieves the possibility of expressing itself in the present progressive, we will be living in the here and now. This will imply loosening the shackles of standardization.

The carnival is a "memento vivere": it reminds us that we need to live and celebrate the voyage of life with dignity, integrity, solidarity, love and tenderness. It is also a practice that can transform itself into a politics of the common good.

17

ART OPERATES like a symbolic appropriation of reality. The act of representing reality or mediating our relation with the world—through an object or product of symbolic art—reinforces the process of reification. Art is a representation that replaces reality. In this same way it is a form of mediation of social and intersubjective relations. Said mediation is produced through cognitive reason, which filters the modes of appreciation of reality. Becoming familiar with reality, the subject internalizes it. This is an appropriation that occurs, straining reality through a utilitarian and functional sieve. The codes of the filter are the codes of instrumental rationality, which projects the expansion of the subject's interiority over the world's exteriority. This develops the cognitive mechanisms of appropriation, categorization, and control of the other—that which is always unknown and unfamiliar. These mechanisms are the product of fear of the outside. Because of this, the projection of interiority upon the exterior world produces an expansive and colonizing zeal. This zeal in turn projects the ego over the other: the external world (nature), and the creatures that inhabit it (human beings, animals, plants, and the soil). The expansive projection of the "I" over nature accelerates the process of reification.

Kant was enraptured by the majestic spectacle of nature. This emotion produced in him a kind of "mental agitation," which he called "sublime." But this emotion is also the living experience of the dread that is sublimated through art, the petrification of the natural spectacle of the world. When art is an institution or a mere object—symbolic and separated from life—it is converted into a symbol of the process of reification. Sophisticated meta-art is nothing more than a symbol of the symbol, a reification of reification. This process sharpens the ideological mechanism of the reification of the subject itself, which, when commodified, alienates itself from reality and loses perspective.

To replace instrumental reason with aesthetic reason does not mean simply replacing the mechanisms of reification. Reification in art exists because art symbolizes that which has been taken from life—the experience of beauty. Art and life have been divided into two separate planes, without any real interconnection. This makes art an institution of the sublime, while life is the praxis of enslavement. Art has been the pressure release valve of alienation. Traditionally it has sheltered those values and energies distanced from life, permitting the maintenance throughout "history" of the illusion of humanity. The separation between art and reality has created a situation in which both planes of experience are lived as isolated spheres, without spirit or emotion. Art becomes petrified in museums, in galleries, in salons and libraries, while existence continues to the rhythm of the minute hand that subjugates salaried work. There, beauty is supressed, joy domesticated, pleasure enslaved, and peculiarity made uniform. Art is the negative mirror of reality that compensates for the miseries of life with the illusion of liberty. To remove art from the sphere of the institution means living art in life and vice versa. It means destroying the alienation that implies the distinction between the artistic and intellectual, and the vulgar and manual. It means beautifying life and enlivening art, both as a unified and organic whole. It also means creating a humanity of artists, and humanizing the artists who already exist.

18

I N EVERY epoch militants have wondered what the revolution will be like and what will happen after it comes to pass. Maybe this future—near or immediate—will not be as bloody or implacable as some prophets have visualized it. Maybe it will be as calm as a fertile and fresh stream, as a meadow. Maybe it will be like a garden cultivated with patience and hands that distinguish the peculiarity of every strain of plant.

The garden of peculiarities manifests itself in a way that some confuse with identity. Identity conforms itself in a reflexive and reactive way with relation to models that integrate dominant indentifying categories. These categories form parts of a map: the North-South axis, Latin America, Africa, First World, etc. These are the symbolic categories of civilizing order. In the same way, these categories are constructed according to structural patterns. This is how standardization functions. Identity then reflects a series of other identities that are erected as paradigms, but which in practice are imposed on the subject without prior warning: nationality, race, class, sexuality, ideology, language, mother, father, etc. These notions—generally taken for granted and which the individual learns almost through osmosis—are the labels of standardization.

Identity is the act of identifying with something, making oneself identical, whether it be a type, model, norm, pattern, level, or reference. Standardization adjusts itself to the model; it typifies. Peculiarity, on the other hand, delves into those subjective zones that situate the subject as a whole that inhabits totality and relates with as many other subjects as there are peculiarities. The notion of peculiarity dismantles the structure of power, which promotes homogenization and authoritarianism because it does not fit in the hierarchical order or the sickness of competition. The subject is capable of relating to all of the other creatures of the planet without the necessity of standardizing anyone. Recognzing peculiarity in other creatures permits coexistence. It dispels the mental module molded by the iron mask of instrumental reason. If one carefully observes the peculiarity of another, the subject does not complete the process of *otherization* because the understanding that the other is as peculiar as oneself, who constitutes the subject and the totality, is revealed. To recognize that the other is nothing more than an I, another peculiar being that also exists in the world, is liberating.

Through *otherization*, the other is reified, whether a human, or the environment. This mechanism of reification fragments the internal subject, displaced from its totality since birth. When the self and everything conform into one totality, reification disappears. Then, the subject—which constitutes the peculiarity of a being—learns the magic of artistic appreciation. This substitutes the module of instrumental reason and poses a new challenge: aesthetic reason.

This does not negate the necessity of creating identity blocks in order to resist the cutural, economic, and military penetration of the civilizing order. In fact—from a political point of view—subordinate identities and liberation movements exist. Clear examples are the movements of the ethnic minorities in the First World, the indigenous movement in Latin America, movements for the liberty of sexual choice, the feminist movement, the workers movement, separatist and anti-neocolonial movements, the urban anarchist resistance, the squatters movement, movements against neoliberal globalization, the ecological and green movement, human rights organizations, artistic movements, rebel movements, etc. In other words, problematizing identity as a notion is arguable from the point of view of anti-authoritarian movements that oppose resistance to the process of standardization. However, from a political point of view as well, it is preferable to understand these movements as constellations of peculiarities inhabiting the garden of reality and resist the sorties of the instrumental steamroller. The ideological machine of standardization homogenizes with its titles of identity. When the garden dismantles hierarchy, every aroma, every color, every form, every taste and every ripple create a landscape whose unique and unrepeatable drive opens the doors to appreciation of beauty. This substitutes the module of instrumental reason for an aesthetic vision that radically displaces the utilitarian and functional logic of the system. It is the first step toward the peculiarization of the world. And it not only opens the mind and disconnects the human brain from the machine of ideology, but it also breaks the shop windows of all commercial chains, negates authority and shouts with a clear and pristine voice, ENOUGH!

19

THE "INSTRUMENTUM" is a mental device that modulates technological thinking. It operates like a tool and makes possible the mechanisms of technical operation. In Greek, the word "technê" has a double meaning: manufacture and revelation. The latter is the capacity to make the present apparent. For Heidegger, "technê" leads in two directions: toward technology or toward "poiêsis." Art also makes the present apparent, but without the instrumental logic of efficiency, or the economic ideology of competition and comparison, whose core is based on transactions.

When art is removed from the institutional sphere to be reinstalled in the praxis of life, there will no longer be a separation between life and art. Of course, life should be lived as if it is a work of art. And art should be experienced in life: not in salons, libraries, museums, or the mausoleum-homes of the ultra rich. When art is practiced in life—and vice versa—there is no need for developing a "sui generis" art market that promotes the mass production of art through mechanical means. Art is realized in an artisanal form, and it implies a genuine aesthetic appreciation. This appreciation is nothing more than the manifestation of a mental module different from instrumentalization that, in a certain sense, can still resuscitate the illusion of humanity. In the same way, aesthetic reason can be a hope. Otherwise, every other path—be it the freeways of instrumental reason or the prehistoric cavern birthplaces of symbolic, representational art—leads to total destruction; avoiding reification is desiring life. The representation of reality—as mediation between nature and consciousness—produces a reifying effect. Total reification occurs when this representation substitutes for reality. And so initiates an infinitely reifying escalation that is only stopped by death.

Symbolic art transformed artisanal aesthetic practice into a fetish, creating distance between "poiêsis" (the act of creation of the appearance of the present) and life (where the creative act expresses itself). By maintaining art and life in dissimilar spheres, instrumental thinking divests life of certain basic values like solidarity, integrity, dignity, tenderness, etc. In fact, sometimes it is only possible to find said values in art or in the vital praxis of unalienated life, fragmenting human life in a radical way and creating the basis for the production of a lucrative artistic market. In this way, the alienation of modern human life justifies itself and denaturalizes everything that comes from nature, naturalizing—as a counterpoint—the pipeline of alienation.

20

IN ORDER to deterritorialize the state it is imperative to oppose militarism and its ideological base—the idea of the nation state. If it were possible to suppress the imaginary of the imagined community, those which exist in the diverse nation-building projects, community would become a real group of people with faces and identifiable names. Its daily interaction would be on a human scale, and the community would truly exist. In this way the state would be deterritorialized.

The idea of the nation state is linked to the idea of race: the foundation of xenophobia and racism. The state has never stopped being a classist and racist instrument of control and oppression. Its territorialization occurs through the movement and deployment of armed forces. In order to dissolve the state it is necessary to dismantle militarism and the arms industry. The state operates as if it were a great national warehouse that invests in warlike exercises: wars. With the dissolution of the state the nation is deterritorialized, and borders lose their reality, becoming what they really are: artificial limits constructed by the high priests of all kinds of nationalisms and regionalisms. These limits are the political bonds imposed by the state on its subjects. Nationalism continues to subjugate people through the sedentary practices derived as much through urban control as through the territorial economy of agriculture. The effect of these practices is domiciliation, which attaches itself to the domesticating action of the state. Notwithstanding, when the apparatus that promotes the concept of national territory dissolves, one of the mechanisms of standardization also stops functioning. To move freely from one zone to another—from community to community—without being subject to customs or police controls, brings with it a freedom that is embodied in daily practice. Constant movement is an uncontrollable force. Its libertarian character is found in its capacity to abolish sedentarism and domiciliation, destroying all state control. To displace oneself is to undomesticate oneself. Going from one place to another, meeting people, learning their languages and understanding different visions of the world is a liberating praxis. This praxis sharpens peculiarity.

Fascism is fomented by nationalism: a feeling of national property exacerbated by the possessing and monied classes. This feeling is transferred to the dispossessed and poor of the cities through the mechanisms of civic, official and national propaganda and indoctrination. Some people, for example, repeat discourses that are spread by ideology in the first person plural. The verb is conjugated as "we," promoting an idiomatic control and reinforcing identifications between country, flag, government and people. To say, for example, "*we* have a park, a mountain range, a good sports team, or a stable economy," implies a kind of linguistic acceptance of an imposed and/or assigned collective national identity. This is the royal *we*, adapted to modern times to make the people think that the government and its financial institutions represent the common individual.

People speak of the actions of the government as if they have had some participation in governmental decisions or in the use of military repression. This is the nationalist alienation that facilitates the appearance of fascism. Indoctrination is reproduced through schools, sports, traditional values, rules, official narratives and means of control. Propaganda is brought to life through luminous screens (television, movies, information technology, etc.), the press, radio, education, etc. Fascism is crystallized through the notion of nation. Because of this, all assigned and/or imposed notions of community identity tend to reinforce said notions: nationality, regionalism, language, social role, professional relationships, religious beliefs, familial clans, brotherhoods and orders, work relationships, job or profession, etc.

Real community does not walk the path of these applied identities. Real community has to do with camaraderie and friendship. And it isn't difficult to imagine. Those who constitute it are those family and friends we see daily and with whom we prefer to relate and enjoy every day. There, everyday solidarity is experienced and the presence of the state is negated. There, mutual recognition and true respect exist. There also, borders are deterritorialized, and the torpid banners of xenophobia are bravely repelled.

21

DRUGS are the only taxonomy possible. There are two kinds of drugs: chemical and natural. The former depend on mass industrial production. The latter are part of nature. They are cultivated, harvested or found in open country (plains, mountains or desert). Through the use of natural drugs humans are able to revisit a time of ancestral wisdom when natural and holistic medicine was practiced. Use of chemical drugs, on the other hand, grew with the industrial revolution and with the ascent of scientific medical doctors to power. This was beginning of the tyranny of the men in white labcoats. Chemical drugs control patience, rhythm and passion. Their objective is to make sure that the dysfunctional subject readjusts itself to the system in order to continue producing submissively. If perchance the white-toga'd priests fail in this attempt and lose control of the patient, their treatment of last resort is to throw the patient into those ideological centers of social reclusion: mental hospitals, hospices, shelters, old folks' homes, etc. These centers are the refuse dumps of terminal illness.

Legal chemical drugs—administered by the state through its health ministries—have as their twin illegal chemical drugs. Besides being a lucrative business, these drugs allow the state to justify repression in zones considered by the state to be out of control: urban ghettoes, marginal neighborhoods or the guerrilla's jungle. In other cases, illegal hard drugs are used as pretexts when "justice" and its Praetorian Guard pursue individuals who are subverting the dominant order. It is exactly the illegality of these drugs that generates large profits and rationalizes authoritarianism.

Natural drugs, on the other hand, liberate because they allow one to see in the darkness of alienation. They help the body. They are biodegradable and are sources of energy. The hemp plant, for example, is a source of rebellion against the very industries that exercise ideological and energy control. The pharmacological industry imposes one vision of reality. Then, the petroleum, mining and forestry industries—the triumvirate of the society of production and mass consumption—carry out the material concretization of this vision of reality. Natural drugs, on the other hand, are curative. While any alteration in consciousness in highly alienated societies provides an escape hatch that allows individuals to appreciate nature, in primitive societies—neither alienated nor alienating—natural drugs are a ratification of the fact that reality is not linear, nor does it manifest itself on only one plane. In effect, through natural drugs primitive communities have experienced the multiple character of reality. As the earth is not flat, neither is reality singular. Rather it is populated by as many folds and multiplicities as nature has peculiarities. The surrealists pointed out that the dream world is also part of reality, just as much as the waking world. The possibility that there are other worlds, without three-dimensional linear logic, has been proven through the use of psychedelics. The experts and doctors—those who work for the society of production and mass consumption—call any attempt to alter the perception of reality through natural drugs escapism. When the escape toward the appreciation of nature becomes an energetic force, the experts and doctors leave their work in the hands of the army or police. This is the so-called war on drugs.

Natural drugs are highly subversive. Every leaf or blade that liberates and alleviates already exists in the planetary garden. Thus, there is no reason to manufacture them. It is a fact that ancestral wisdom is related to natural medicine. Many women were accused of being witches—by the doctors and experts of their times—and burned alive at the stakes of the Catholic, Protestant and patriarchical Inquisition. That's civilization.

Eating, smoking, boiling and swallowing natural drugs are acts of shared solidarity. The occurrence of these acts depends on the health of people. When the rhythm of life is controlled by the automated tic-tac of the standardizing machine, the general level of health is diminished.

Alienation and ideology are a sickness. Natural drugs weed the garden and work the soil. Every time natural drugs—organic like we are—are ingested, we recuperate from the biological and social diseases produced by alienation and ideology. Humanity needs to recover from the trauma of civilization. For Chellis Glendinning, civilization is a state from which one needs to get better. The trauma of the first day of classes, the nervousness provoked by the threat of expulsion from school, stomach pains, irrational punishments, or the impact of institutional repression against the libertarian manifestation of the being that wants to flee from alienation and ideology, are all consequences of a traumatic experience that we try to ignore day in and day out. Civilization is the foundation of the forced training that privileges the symbolic over the imaginary in order to break the state of natural "savagery" that we all inhabit.

Natural drugs unfold the petals of the imagination. This might be the effect we produce ourselves everytime we interact organically with the environment and we expand our universe toward that which we haven't yet dreamed, but can imagine. Our presence has a hallucinogenic effect. We are, in effect, a powerful drug that can illuminate everything we imagine. And once we are liberated, there is no chemical drug, nor screen, nor army that can stop the enticing and opiating effect of our own presence. In order to construct a new world it is necessary to imagine it. And to imagine it, it is necessary to liberate oneself. This liberation entails the creation of a new humanity. This is the importance of natural drugs.

22

THE IMPACT of human life on the planet and all other living creatures is inescapable. The consequences of every single life are inevitable: we walk and we destroy. The destructive effect produced by our existence is amplified by instrumental reason. Instrumental reason is nothing less than a mental module that operates like bewildering ideology: it permits neither feeling nor understanding. Once entrapped in this framework, consciousness rolls up like petrified tissue. In order to sensitize oneself, it is necessary to explore the aesthetic. Art and poetry help us to see in the midst of alienation. Abolishing instrumental reason does not mean abolishing logical or analogical thinking, and even less so intelligence and practical capability. Analogy and logic coexist in nature and in the human mind as an inseparable whole. To associate, for example, the chirping of crickets with the purring of nature, like a happy and satisfied cat, is part of aesthetic thinking. Analogy is manifested through logical, intellectual and linguistic procedures, but its approach is aesthetic before it is instrumental, privileging the appreciation of the natural world and its beauty instead of the functionality of what can be extracted from nature. In order to abolish instrumental reason it is necessary to de-alienate oneself and to unlearn ideological and social training. This is a challenge that must be focused on dismantling the tool that permits this training: the language that constitutes the subject.

Without language the notion of the subject vanishes. Instrumental, aesthetic and ethical reason—divided in separate spheres between economics and politics, art and poetry, ethics and religion—permitted the appearance of language. Instrumental reason, however, took control of language, thus generating the forms of exploitation of humans and nature imposed by civilization through a sophisticated system of division of labor. Anthropologists believe that that moment was the beginning of history, of agriculture and sedentarism. It may also have been the beginning of the slow process of the objectification of the subject and the acceleration of the expansive motion of civilization rationalized through the notion of progress. The Socratic maxim "know thyself" caused the subject to philosophically reify itself in order to transform itself into its own object of study. In addition, this meant the dissection and separation of the subject from reality; it converted itself into an entity apart, different and estranged from the whole formed by nature.

23

JOHN ZERZAN argues that language appropriates reality in order to later replace it. According to anarcho-primitive thinking, the division of labor produces a reifying sequence that ends with the creation of the symbolic. For Zerzan, the symbolic not only represents reality, but also replaces it. This substitution is a form of alienation and constitutes the beginning of civilization, where instrumental reason amplifies the mechanisms of control of language, standardardizing absolutely everything and completely rejecting any peculiarity. In this way reality is transformed into a set of objects, whereby the subject is one more object that fits in the box of a category. Civilization and alienation are then two cysts of the same nature that must be removed.

24

I N 1987, J.A. Lagos Nilsson published in Buenos Aires the anarchist manifesto *"Contracultura y provocación"* (Counterculture and Provocation), in opposition to the hackneyed terms culture and civilization, terms which were utilized by the dictatorships of Argentina and Chile to justify themselves and rationalize their genocidal practices. For Lagos Nilsson, the cultural world is a model, a pattern, a frame, or a reference: it is what standardizes. In this way, standardizing culture and civilization are a product of the expansion of instrumental reason, which is manifested psychologically as the projection of the ego over nature. Alienation produces the estrangement of the subject from the world, causing the subject to become strange to the external world and to him or herself. This is the sickness that is transmitted in the pipeline of ideology. In this whirlwind, only art and poetry liberate and de-alienate. This liberating action is rooted in the counterculture, which is nothing more than a form of a meaningful provocation. For obvious reasons, the counterculture negates the official culture and advocates for the right of peculiarity. Clearly then, counterculture does not makes pacts or coexist with power, although the latter tries to co-opt the former. If it achieves co-option, counterculture becomes nothing more than a fetish of consumption, or a museum piece that power hangs on the lapel of its jacket like a military medal.

Power perpetuates itself through the practice of repression and the sickness of alienation. If it's true that alienation is a practice of the symbolic, it still is not necessarily an expression of symbolic culture. The distinction between the symbolic and symbolic culture permits one to distinguish between representation and the reifying substitution of reality, and the aesthetic manifestation of being. Confusing civilization with culture means mixing two equidistant manifestations. Civilization is the projection of instrumental reason. Its most sublime expression is embedded in the cities, which, legitimized as second nature, organize the process of ideological and social training in modern subliminal concentration camps. Culture, instead, when it emanates from the subject, is a form of being, or a counterculture. Culture regulates itself through the interaction of being. In civilization, on the other hand, whose game board of interaction is the market, true self-regulating mechanisms do not exist, since its base of support is utility, profit and usury. Civilization is, therefore, one-dimensional. In contrast, culture is multiple, peculiar and multifaceted. What orients the forms of cultural manifestation is being. Doing relates to manipulation and production. And while this can be a creative act, it is profoundly tied to instrumental functionality. Being and creation interweave the thread of culture. Truly, we all have culture, that is, a way of being. And if it's true that culture mediates our experience, then our being is cultural.

The struggles of the indigenous communities in Latin America are nothing less than the battle for the defense of their culture against the penetration of the civilizing machine and standardizing culture. The culture of a community is the aesthetic manifestation of its communitarian being. This is symbolic culture.

Neanderthal men and women, who disappeared approximately thirty thousand years ago, created polished rock figurines and constructed flutes from bear bones which were capable of playing as many as three musical notes: do, re, mi. They also had a form of communication and spiritual and artistic activities. Symbolic culture does not necessarily drive down a civilizing highway with no exit. The Maya, for example, abandoned their cities without any explanation. It is likely that they had understood in some moment, that their civilization was not sustainable, although there is no concrete proof of that. It is also possible that they had a clear understanding that the technology that they would develop would be so drastic that they would not be able to return to the earth what they had taken from it. This cosmology of retribution still forms a part of the symbolic culture of the Maya, whose understanding of nature easily surpasses the modern western cosmologies.

In contrast with the Mayan culture, western civilization and its replicas have provoked nothing but the accelerated destruction of nature. When Marcuse proposes that history negates nature, he refers to civilizing culture—standardization—and not human culture as the expression of being. The manifestation of being is aesthetic and cultural. This manifestation turns radical when it becomes the peculiar expression of being. For this reason, to negate a person's way of being is to colonize him or her. This practice reproduces the expansive impulse of civilization, which is nothing more than the destruction of nature and human beings. Civilization, therefore, colonizes and domesticates culture, reducing it to a standard category—the official culture. To not recognize that every creature on the planet has a manner of being—every cat, bird, plant, flower, ourselves—is to negate the peculiarity of nature.

To negate culture is to standardize. Human beings have different ways of being. Everyone sees, feels and appreciates the world culturally. Every culture is peculiar. Constellations of peculiarities are cultural forms that turn into the idiosyncrasies of subjects.

The genocides and ecocides of the North and South American continents have moved in one main direction: to negate indigenous culture. Culture, indeed, is counter to civilization. They are not synonymous, but distinct territories. Civilization implies standardization; culture, peculiarity.

25

LANGUAGE fulfills a double function: it standardizes and imposes meaning, but it also liberates. Through language, the subject resists the objectification produced by instrumental reason through its standardizing practices: ideological categories, industrial monoculture, ranching, etc.

Conversation de-alienates and congregates, dismantling the systemic politics that tends toward individual isolation. Standardization, in contrast, cretinizes. In order to do this, it simplifies language, reducing our capacity to recognize reality. This simplification reduces itself to the Orwellian newspeak, which reduces consciousness and atrophies imagination. The subject is not consciousness in itself, just as language is not in itself communication. If we trust the results of science, it is possible to establish that writing appeared sixty thousand or more years ago. The calcareous marks left by Australian aborigines on rocks are proof of this. Obviously, this is not western writing, but the marks are meaning-carrying graphic inscriptions. It is also probable that language has always accompanied human beings, whether it was a form of guttural verbalization, which little by little became more clearly articulated, or as simple gestural communication. Some anthropological texts argue that language and symbolic thinking have existed for millions of years. The stone tools, which can be dated at two and a half million years, are evidence of the existence of rational mechanisms not only related to the symbolic, but also to biped biological evolution, to the use of the thumb and group organization. Marcel Griaule shows that for the members of the African Dogon community, from Mali, the first word enunciated by human beings was "breath." This suggests that the origin of language was not articulation, but breath itself. In effect, the peculiarity of speaking is characterized by the biorhythm of inhalation and exhalation in every human body. Speaking is as proper to and unique as the accent each one of us has in our own language.

The subject organizes its personality structurally. In this way the subject annuls consciousness, although it can also amplify consciousness through language. To create consciousness, therefore, means realizing our existence in the totality of the cosmos. Through consciousness we create the world. That is, we mark and point out events or issues which otherwise would remain in darkness or silence. Alienation, on the contrary, blinds, causing individuals to follow a track wearing blinders or to be enclosed in cubicles. Language is, therefore, a tool of indoctrination, but also a weapon of liberation. Under the present conditions of human, animal and ecological domestication, the alienating separation of the subject from totality can be seen as an irreversible process. Returning to a primitive state prior to articulated language implies unlearning languages (this is practically impossible without eliminating human beings from the face of the planet). Abolishing the notion of language, even without an exhaustive genocide of all humanity, is an unrealizable and sinister project. What's more, there is no guarantee that the instrumental aspect of symbolic thinking would not reappear at some moment in the development of life. And with it would resurge new forms of alienation and functional domination over nature and the normalizing control of human beings. Hoping for, thus, a utopian, synthetic construction of a primitive communist order based on hunting and gathering, which by extension guarantees the survival of only the strongest and replaces language with telepathy, also seems unlikely.

Life has lost its value through the symbolic control of instrumental reason. In alienated and alienating societies, only art and poetry can return the original value of life, given that the aesthetic sphere has been separated from the range of the vital. This separation is nothing more than a strategy of compensation for what has been lost. In order for art to give value back to life, it is necessary to destroy the divisive line between symbolic creation and existence, mixing life and the aesthetic in a single cycle. Thus, combating the symbolic with the symbolic implies a contradiction, but also the possibility of ideological emancipation and the abolition of instrumental reason. Orienting human activities toward aesthetic reason can correct the course of life across the planet and save many creatures— and ourselves—from total extinction.

26

THE SLOVAKIAN SLAVOJ ZIZEK states that every ecological project oriented toward changing technology to improve the state of our natural environment delegitimates itself, in as much as every initiative of this kind trusts in the very source of the problem—the technological mode of relating ourselves to the other entities in our surroundings. This is the same contradiction that is repeated in combating the symbolic with the symbolic: writing, articulated thought, language. Both contradictions, however, are false because they act as systemic traps that promote inaction: silence in one case, complacency in the other. Truly, the effects of human life on the planet are unavoidable: we walk and we destroy, we breathe and we annihilate. This destructive impact is amplified through instrumental reason: the technological mode of relating ourselves to the other entities in our surroundings. And it is multiplied by the mechanisms of mass production and mechanical reproduction. Instrumental reason is, therefore, a functional and bewildering ideology that uproots the aesthetic from life by virtue of imposing a civilizing project on the planet. This project mediates social, human and animal life through domestication. Instrumental reason is an ideological taming that puts people to sleep, makes them apathetic, erases the imagination and atrophies the senses. When wild animals are tamed, they stop being animals and become domestic beings—pets. To be domesticated and dominated is to be imprisoned in the domus: an architectural repetition that standardizes the landscape. The domus of wild animals is the corral, ranch, stable, hogshed. The human domus is a solitary room or a set of rooms shared by roommates that draws the gray panorama of the city.

Alienation in the cities—social spaces on the verge of fatal collapse—and the destruction engendered by mass production are defining characteristics of life under the control of the domesticating action of instrumental reason. Aesthetic reason does not propose human dominion over nature. On the contrary, it foresees human existence in a mode that is interdependent with and in nature, without any control. Life is a flexible and organic net of daily events. Aesthetic reason broadens consciousness, amplifies the imagination and promotes integrity and responsibility as necessary ethics. It is a project that does not lack elasticity, or practical sense, or intelligence. But it privileges the artistic over the functional. Its purpose, then, is the radical unfurling of all the anti-authoritarian peculiarities that inhabit the planet.

A world oriented toward aesthetic reason suggests a communal and artisanal lifestyle. The cosmovision that integrates such reason is biocentric. It weeds out the anthropocentrism from the planetary garden and deposits enlightened humanism in the compost bin. Biocentrism is nothing more than the realization that life is the sphere that includes reality, without discounting that other realities and perceptions of reality exist. The garden of peculiarities is a project of humanity: to build life in a planetary garden populated by nonhierarchical, autonomous and liberatarian communities that operate on the basis of analogical and aesthetic thinking. Analogy permits the establishment of associations and connections in simultaneous, multiple, flexible, transparent and interdependent forms, dismantling linear logic and isolation—all on the same flank—in order to combat all the perverse forms of alienation. Maybe in this garden it will be possible to fully communicate with each other by means of certain faculties that have been lost through and atrophied by domestication. Maybe we will develop other senses.

Hens, for example, are able to recognize up to fifty members of their community. Their organizational system is based on mutual recognition. In this way, they avoid any conflicts over feed and establish a social dynamic based on empathy with other hens, giving preference to older birds while pecking. With industrial domestication, chicken farms were filled with hundreds of hens that were forced to forget their natural wisdom and not recognize the other members of their species, awakening violence, if not insanity. We human beings have lost and forgotten our natural wisdom. The Australian aborigines that still walk about the desert are able to communicate telepathically at distances of up to several kilometers. When poetry and art become an asystemic counterideology, our faculties reawaken. Then we are able to create the world and freely express the peculiarity that the system negates. Some peculiarities have more open petals than others. This has no importance. Equalizing standardization is a socioliberal trick that cynically denies social egalitarianism, given that it exists by virtue of hierarchical differences. What is important is that every petal opens, at its own rhythm and under its own conditions, establishing an intimate synchronicity with the world of living beings. The equalizing machine is unjust to peculiarity. Life is an energy that permits the re-creation of the world into different peculiar worlds. The free creation of constellations of peculiarities—free association, in socioliberal parlance— is a notion that can help to better describe the conditions of life under the influence of the organic movement of self-sufficient communities. These communities flourish on gregarious living together—sociality, in socioliberal terms—and allow the peculiarity of each creature to blossom. This flowering is the total and liberating unfurling of our being, and permits an organic interaction between human beings and the planet.

In the garden of peculiarities, flowers and plants realize the process of photosynthesis to the rhythm of their own sap. No one stops them. Nobody slows them down. Nobody speeds them up or controls them. Animals and insects that sneak through the garden cross the ephemeral heartbeat of the present. And so is the perpetual motion of the earth kept alive. And so persists the planet: the astral domus that provides us shelter and keeps us alive.

27

WERE THERE anthropophagous practices during the hunting-gathering stage of human development or even earlier? Has human meat been the alimentation of other humans? Do we have a cannibal past? It seems that the answer is yes, although we do not know if cannibalism has been practiced toward the end of human survival, or as a purely symbolic practice.

The study of molars in human craniums and tooth marks on human bones found in caves in Great Britain demonstrates that the ancestors of the English were cannibals. In the seventeenth and eighteenth centuries the doctors at some European courts prescribed a diet of human organs to cure certain diseases. Organ banks were not uncommon during that epoch, and neither were the executions that were necessary to fill the storehouses with kidneys, livers, intestines and other human parts needed to satisfy the appetites of courtiers hungry to cure what ailed them. The use of the guillotine slowed at the same moment when Europe erased its anthropophagous history and began a new stage: attributing cannibalism to conquered peoples, which were seen either as noble savages or dangerous barbarian "man-eaters."

In the novel *El Entenado*, based on the memories of the Spaniard Francisco del Puerto (who arrived on the east coast of the Southern Cone with the expedition of Díaz de Solís in 1516), Juan José Saer narrates in beautiful prose the experience of a captive in Guarani territory.

Indo-American cannibalism was not sustained toward the necessity of survival, but as a symbolic ritual: to distinguish the other from the "we" and so affirm the precarious order of the universe. Every time that the Tupis Guaranis staged a "meat festival"—or carnival—they reaffirmed their role in the preservation of the fragile cosmic balance. This ethnic and anthropocentric vision, filtered through cannibal practice, had nothing more than a symbolic and ceremonial purpose—to assert that the true people did not eat each other. Indeed, the cannibals only tasted strangers or others who, in the eyes of the ethnocentric village, did not exist or form part of the true people. The dialectic exercised between cannibalism and group self-identification, as a strategy of identity construction, would have been the base of all symbolic expression. The notion of "we" is distinguished in this way from the notion of "them." And this distinction is ratified in ritual through cannibalistic practice. It is, in a certain light, a mythology that explains the cosmos and fixes a conviction of belonging, which is otherwise unarticulated. This might be what Francisco del Puerto witnessed during the nearly ten years he spent in capitivity. And this is the reason why the Charrúas (the Guarani) of the Plata River kept him in captivity. A witness to the cannibalistic act was necessary to ratify the existence of the Guaranis among the inhabitants of other villages. But for the Spanish empire, cannibalism was used as an argument to demonize indigenous cultures and so justify their blood-soaked genocide.

The notion of "we" proceeds from another earlier notion—the "I." The notion of the "I" rises from the consciousness of our own mortal condition, which foresees a hypothetical, future and dauntless situation—death. That visualization of the future is that which separates human consciousness from the survival instinct, or hypersensitivity to risk, or any other animal consciousness.

When the Spanish soldier Bernal Díaz del Castillo entered under orders of Hernán Cortés into the city of Tenochtitlán, constructed on Lake Texcoco, his amazement of the marked and imperial grandeur of the Aztecs was diminished by the terror he felt in the presence of human cadavers piled inside the Aztecs' sacred temples. The Aztecs did not only practice human sacrifices; they were also cannibals. In his narrative, Bernal Díaz remembers when Moctezuma is served on his royal plate tiny humans, nothing more than children and babies. In this way, Bernal Díaz demonizes the other and scandalizes the Spanish, whose fear finds voice in religious discourse. The distinction that the Europeans made establishes the difference between "they" and "we." That is, between barbarity—atheist or possessed, fomenting anthropophagy—and Catholic civilization, notwithstanding that Catholics also symbolically eat and drink the body of Christ. This reasoning is utilized by the empire to justify the genocide that occurred in the Americas and thus reaffirm the supposed right of conquest. The Christian cross and the liturgy are still symbolic forms of sacrifice and cannibalism. The sacrifices and anthropophagous practices of the Aztecs were symbolic forms of identity, culture and collective reaffirmation and were a direct consequence of their cosmovision.

Other South American peoples also practiced ritual sacrifices, although it is still an open question whether or not they were cannibals. These sacrifices were offerings to the Gods. Their objective was to give sustenance to the spirit of the elements in return for protection. The Mapuches of southern Chile—one of the few peoples not conquered by the Spanish—sacrificed lambs in ritual healing ceremonies. The witchdoctor—or *machi*—extracted the heart of the animal and bathed in its blood. This was nothing more than a symbolic act of redemption before the forces of nature. The symbolic appears with the rise of consciousness, represented by death. The recognition of our mortal condition would be the generating impulse in the creation of our notion of the human and the nonhuman, of the animate and the inanimate, of the raw and cooked. In such a context, cannibalism and animal sacrifice were the reaffirmation of the human. Eating the other, whether human or animal, was to ratify the existence of a "we": the primitive horde or the original tribe.

Freud suggests that civilization is based in the repressed, in the taboos of cannibalism and incest. This repression is the origin of the bases of western civilization. The civilized is the repressed. Culture also represses, given that it must hide its anthropophagous character: plagiarism, citation, and mere reference. Symbolically, culture swallows itself in a net of connections that expand in a chain reaction. Mercantile and enslaving vampirism is culturally based on a cannibalistic drive whose most appropriate representation is found in the popular expression, "suck the blood of others," that is, of the dominated. Of course, when culture represents cannibalism, it does so with the filter of the spectacle. It makes cannibalism into a caricature or gives it aberrant characteristics. It is a "naked tango" or the distortion of an individual who has lost all sense of humanity. In the first case, cannibalism is a spectacle that contradicts the dance of the flesh. When the Guaranis staged their bacchanals, they did it to the rhythm of dance and drums, and it was supposed to be a celebratory remembrance of their own humanity. While Christians awaited Lent, they staged a carnival, another form of "meat festival," but one that was sublimated by the symbolic. The "naked tango" is a stylized, but also raw, drama of the anthropophagous act. It is manifested in fascism, torture and humiliation. On the other hand, the image of the cannibal as an individual aberration is an ideological trick that reinforces the propaganda that fosters self-control, self-censorship, and oppressive force. In both cases, it represses the multiple peculiarity that inhabits nature. That is the veil that negates the origin of the idea of humanity.

It is probable that symbolic culture and its reifying ramifications have come from a first consciousness, the certainty of death. This certainty generates, through the self-reflexive mechanisms of consciousness, the recognition of our own existence. This carries with it a vision of an "I-we," in opposition to an "other-them." In this sense, cannibalism was the symbolic affirmation of the belligerent cosmovision between the notions of "us" and "them."

Selective anthropophagy (eating the stranger but not the neighbor) is the primordial establishment of a differentiating and rationalized self-conscious revulsion that mediates the notion of the human and nonhuman. It is not certain, in any case, that humans are carnivorous. In fact, all indications point to the contrary. We are herbivorous, vegetarian, or vegans who still eat meat or have barbecues as a form of metabolic inertia owing to a diet imposed ancestrally for symbolic reasons. When the eater eats nonhuman meat, the reward is the status of human.

Geographic variants also have influenced regional diets. The food supply of the Eskimos, for example, is nearly a hundred percent carnivorous. However, their location in a region where survival is difficult is due to a previous displacement, determining their diet. Many nomadic peoples kept themselves in motion following the routes of buffaloes or other animals. Maritime resources caused many tribal groups to settle in polar areas and dedicate themselves to fishing as a prolongation of an older carnivorous practice. This was also the case with the Alacalufes or Selknam in South America. Today they have totally disappeared.

To assume our animal nature implies understanding that modern society is reproducing an ancestral form of cannibalism. We are animals that eat other animals. We are herbivorous animals that eat the meat of others. Of course the hunting and fishing tribes of the Paleolithic and Neolithic were meat eaters. But those societies had already worked and polished stone, which implies the use of certain techno-instrumental thinking in order to construct tools. It is also probable that this incipient application of instrumental reason came after the appearance of consciousness—the realization of our own death. It is also probable that instrumentality came after the rise of the notions of a collective "I" and a collective "you." Said notions are the embryonic forms of cannibalism, which is nothing more than a symbol of the ratification of community identity in the primitive horde, in the clan and the tribe. In this sense, it is probable that the consumption of nonhuman meat has perpetuated a symbolic mechanism of self-affirmation that was imposing, little by little—and maybe for reasons of survival—the carnivorous diet on beings with flat teeth and porous skin.

28

PHYSIOLOGICALLY, humans are herbivorous beings. We do not have claws, and we perspire through pores—in contrast with carnivores, which perspire through the tongue—and our small incisors are not sharp like those of carnivorous animals. What's more, we have flat molars for chewing and grinding and our intestines are twelve times length than the total of our body, similar to other herbivores, the longitude of whose intestines fluctuates between ten and twelve times the body length. If we compare this with the intestines of carnivores, the extension of whose intestines is only three times the length of the body—which permits the rapid processing of decomposing meat through the digestive system—and the presence of strong stomach acids that help to digest meat, acids which are twenty times more potent that the acids present in the stomachs of humans and herbivores, then we see that there are no physiological reasons to suppose that humans need to eat meat. The reasons for our carnivorism are ideological. And they tend to justify human supremacy over the animal world.

Michael Klaper asserts that humans are not carnivores, either by anatomy or nature. In one of his books on the vegan diet, he shows that human beings cannot effectively eat raw meat with pleasure—in the case that we would do that—and he contrasts the pleasure of eating a raw apple, watermelon or salad with the carnivorous act, which generally requires seasoning and cooking in order to render it as far as possible from its real nature: dead flesh and nerves. In this sense, the carnivorous diet is a kind of necrophagy, which has been socially imposed, and which derives from anthropophagous practice. Both diets are nothing more than acts of symbolic ritual. Cannibalism served as a rite of distinction between tribal identity and the identity of others while carnivorism was a ceremony necessary to distance humans from animals. In effect, through carnivorism, an anthropocentric vision that ideologically guarantees the "superiority" of humans over animals and morally justifies human control over nature has been perpetuated. In both cases comestibles are objectified. And in both cases there are symbols and reification.

Prehistoric hunting tribes expanded their territory looking for animals to hunt. They chiseled and polished stones as weapons of defense and attack. They designed stalking, territorial control and assault tactics. This was the base of the development of the logic of instrumental aggression that gave rise to combat and hoarding. But it wasn't a homogenous process. The Indians of the North American plains, for example, respected the buffalo—which was sacred in their cultures—and they did not mutilate it on a massive scale, nor did they domesticate it. In carnivorous civilizations, however, this first expansive movement still persists. It is a fact that hunting is one of the cornerstones over which the foundations of carnivorous civilization were raised. The murderous irrationality of civilization operates as a parallel with human irrationality. In effect, we are the only species of animals that, being herbivorous, prefer to nourish ourselves with dead creatures. This is total madness.

29

CURRENT SCIENCE and the dominant cosmology not only look to totally submerge— by representational means—the cannibalistic past of humans, they also have an instrumentalizing functional ingredient. The use of human embryos and fetuses in biogenetic medicine, the use of animal and artificial organs in human implants, the "McDonaldizing" expansion of the carnivorous diet, the biotechnological production of transgendered foods, biopiracy, sport hunting, the buying and selling of newborns, etc. are all ideological modes of the symbolic reconstruction of a new notion of the subject: cyborgs.

Cyborgs are robotized beings that are connected for a greater part of the day to different kinds of machines (computers, televisions, cell phones, answering machines, cars, headphones, escalators, pacemakers, clocks, alarms, etc.). Cyborgs and automatons are a direct consequence of present-day science and modern cosmology. They have no memory because their thinking follows the route programmed by the idea of linear time. They lack spontaneity, although they improvise. Spontaneity arrests their programming because it prioritizes the organic and natural present. Thus, it foresees the discourse of life. Improvisation, on the other hand, is centered in immediate action and does not anticipate the consequences. It is the lucrative logic, cybernetic urgency, and desire for profit.

The cyborg is boring and insincere. It lacks transparency and responsibility. Its food is based on the pure science that fabricates genetically manipulated and modified organisms, hiding what they truly are with their appearance: false legumes, vegetables that are no longer vegetables, plastic foods, canned fruit, and so on. All this responds to a strictly regulated plan for the future and life that accords with models and goals that are also strictly designed. Along the same vein, the cyborg is incapable of discerning the destructive and violent effect of its actions. Rather, it denies it.

In the same way that the carnivorous diet and religion were naturalized cultural interventions—interventions that symbolically represent a form of repression caused by a civilizing action whose end is nothing less than the construction of human identity—so also the sciences and modern machines are naturalized cultural interventions that represent the repression of the notion of humanity and whose end is nothing less than the construction of a world of cyborgs. The cyborg is the model of modern standardization. Its integrity is a double standard: it defends the violence exercised by the repressors, and it attacks the self-defense of the oppressed. Its ideal diet consists of pills. And its ideology is alienation.

30

ANY ATTEMPT at standardization whatsoever is a form of domination because it imposes a single mode of being over peculiarity. Every value-driven or ideological matrix is an example of this domination, given that the only possible integrity is connected to the multiple, simultaneous and peculiar flowering of nature. Standardization is a form of colonization that imposes a unifying pattern over the differences and peculiarities of everyone. Every model hides a system of planning that organizes the model itself. Every plan requires linear temporality in order to "progress" and foster the motion of development. Present-day science and modern dominant cosmology justify the colonization of the peculiarity of nature—people, forests, plants, animals, birds, soil, etc.—by way of the indexes of the so-called "standard of living." Those who accustom themselves to the various standards of living become automatons. The automaton stands in opposition to nature, losing its humanity—maybe constructed by cannibalism in the primitive horde—and winds its memory like a videotape to be re-programmed by the standardizing machine. Later it survives by replaying the same tape. This is boredom. In the same way, the automaton erases its past, is blind to the present and loses its history, which would have been, in other circumstances, ancestral, as it is with other humans. The automaton values only what it remembers: its electronic passwords, its license plate number, the code numbers and barcodes assigned to it by the great machine-mother, etc. It lacks, therefore, history. This is its pride and its perfidy.

31

IN A PLACE in the American Northwest, on the outskirts of Eugene, Oregon, a hippie beanfest is celebrated annually. This fair is not quite a quilombo, although it could be. Quilombos are disordered, rebellious, turbulent and Dionysian. They permit peculiarities to meet in a natural state of anarchy manifested in the perpetual present. Notwithstanding, the beanfest of the Northwest induces every participant to highlight one aspect of their individuality, normed by a varied gamut of previously conformed cultural types: fashion, fetish, appearance. This standardizes the revelry and impedes a true celebration, uniforming the fun. By contrast, the true carnival is a ritual of remembrance, rings the warning bells over our own reality and comprises a primordial knowledge—that human beings are nothing but nature. Death is sufficient demonstration of that. The fair, on the other hand, needs rules, security systems, guards, undercover police, all of which go against nature, the planet and the joyous expression of being. Today, for example, it is illegal to smoke a joint in the fair. But it wasn't always this way. In fact, the Oregon Country Fair began as a sixties festival that wanted to emulate the carnivals of the Middle Ages and was highly anti-establishment in the beginning. Hippies and flower people from all over the world attended, unfolding their colors and rebel smiles against uniformity.

The locals form musical combos, and they play a kind of long folksong that is associated with country music. The curious thing is that they sometimes sing songs that can appear to have too much in common with the lives of their listeners. In reality, this is not strange. It is a product of standardization. The heroes and characters of the songs become stereotypes produced, massified and administrated by the symbolic culture that reproduces control through the image. In this way, standardization appropriates peculiarity and transforms it into a recognizable typology: archetypes, types of physiologies, stereotypes, etc.

Stereotypes are vulgar forms of understanding standardization and exist only by virtue of it. For example, bus drivers always wave to each other when they pass. This happens wherever civilization has had a uniforming and homogenizing impact. The more stereotypes a society has, the higher its level of standardization and alienation. The stereotype is an image charged semiotically and semantically by categories. Its action—which is projected onto reality—is imposed over oppressed groups in the forms of exoticism or demonization. The exotic is a category constructed by the dominant order to infantilize the other and appropriate him or her. Demonization provides self-justification for aggression against the other.

Without categories, the typologies and collective images cannot be widely recognized. Stereotypes spectacularize uniformity. This is obvious in mass culture: in the mass media culture of audiovisual communication or "mainstream" American culture, for example. Its ideology is mediocrity, and its goal is to make sure that all human beings fit like cogs in a big and incomprehensible machine. Toward this end, standardization is a process of human cretinization through the average, standard formats. These formats contain the values of plutocratic democracy that hold the line behind the gains of the "mediocracies." That is to say, the standardizing government and ideologies: democratic concepts that are openly embodied by fascism. For the beanfest to again become some kind of quilombo, it is imperative that all the wild feathers of peculiarity be unfurled. If not, the party is transformed into a concentration camp with confetti and balloons, but without sharing, or laughter, or companionship. This is not very different from what happens at official events, which are repeated over and over again in schools and public and private institutions, labor ceremonies, and so on. Truly, the objective of these pseudo-celebrations is to prepare the ideological and emotional foundation for propagandistic indoctrination and repressive control: the twin weapons that the system uses to maintain immobility. The quilombo, on the other hand—as a true carnival—is a form of social staging of consciousness, whose Dionysian practice liberates and separates the reveler from the machine of training and conduct control. That which is Dionysian, in this case, not only disrupts the culture of "reason," by antithetically opposing itself to the Apollonian, it also dissipates instrumental norms by dismantling the duality between Bacchus and Apollo, which fades away in the rebellious character of the celebration.

32

EVERY REVOLUTION has reforms while, without revolution, reforms never really take place. The means and the ends meet in a perpetual present in which reality, imagination, desire and its realization, art, and life coincide. In the same way, the dividing line that limits the imaginary and the symbolic orders, the organic and the structured, the animated and the totality is erased. This binary combination of different subjects— which generally impose a cover over the consciousness of the understanding of the world— falls apart when one perceives the tactic of immediacy as part of a global strategy. In the same way, the comprehension of totality as an interdependent whole erases the dividing line between liberty and fear, and chips away the shell that separates human beings from the natural world.

The notion of liberty is found on the earth. And behind the steel bars rises the unfortunate experience of the caged prisoner. The revolution must transform daily events into a form of ethics realized in a perennial present. This is a bit speculative, in that it is based in the ethical urgency of transformation. Immobility, in any case, pays homage to repression. Only movement liberates.

33

THE STANDARDIZING system domesticates. Domestication is a form of dominion that turns living creatures into homebodies that laze around in their domus. In this way standardization forces domiciliation, whose culminating expression is found in curfew. Like all systems, this generates its antibodies: the unemployed, who act like a reserve labor army and the homeless, whom the system throws away.

Mass production generates a crisis of overproduction and stagnation: unemployment, poverty, social class distinctions, and so on. In addition, it galvanizes the logic of accumulation and reifying rationality by means of mass media control, producing as a consequence a kind of massive added value of images that reinforce consumption and accelerate accumulation itself.

To dismantle the standardizing system and mass industrial production it is necessary to reconcile two radical points: the means of social relations, and the forms of alimentation and production of necessary items. Clearly, in order to construct a planetary garden, it is a necessity to promote nonhierarchical forms of social relations that spread organically like a net of constellations of peculiarities. That is, as a set of communities or groupings similar to tribal bands. The basis for a system of alimentation should be horticulture and permaculture, practiced in self-sustainable community plots and maintained only and exclusively for local and immediate satisfaction of the community (not for sale, nor for the accumulation of goods or money). It goes without saying that no one should regulate the work of another and all decisions should be made as a group. Responsibility is a conscious act of solidarity. Leisure time should be highly valued, as well as the capacity to appreciate nature and the universe, which are, after all, sources of vital energy. In effect, the heart of the planet and of the cosmos deserve to be celebrated in the every day as well as in the collective. In this way leisure, the aesthetic, and social life can be woven together outside of all hierarchy, constructing a politics based on celebration and a carnivalesque, ritualistic coexistence.

Consumption can be mediated through a kind of cooperative in which the members contribute as they can. Obviously, in the planetary garden there won't be money or any sort of commercial trading that will fuel the value of exchange. Yet the production of manufactured articles is inevitable. We human beings manipulate and make tools. This is the nature of our opposable thumb. That's how it was in the Paleolithic and how it is today. The function of our capacity to grasp objects and create beauty is represented in two vital practices: the gathering of food and the sharing of love when we give and receive caresses. In this sense, the utilization of appropriate technology independent of the processes of mass industrial production could be key in the hour of survival. Engineering based on the human heart, like bicycles or wind or solar energy are concrete alternatives to industrial pollution. If social life is visualized in open communities—in daily contact with nature—the risk of reification dissipates. Nature not only takes care of us, it also frees us and makes us healthy, helping us avoid the traps of alienation.

The word forest comes from the Latin "foris," which means "gateway to open air." Undomestication implies the abandonment of the domus to go deeply into the open air—into the jungle or the forest. This abandonment is the quintessence of all liberation. Thus, crossing the threshhold from immobility means breaking down the doors of the domus and sweeping away all the driveways, eliminating the concrete. It also requires undoing ourselves from all that ties us to the post of civilization, and that not only negates human animality, but it also denies its pleasure-giving and rebellious nature.

34

JOHN TRUDELL proposes the distinction between authority and power to allude to, on the one hand, the nature of the standardizing system embodied in civilization and its domesticating practices, and, on the other, the capacity for resistance against said system. In fact, all authoritarian practice has its roots in the notion of authority, which is nothing more than the exercise of power to subordinate and force obedience to hierarchy. Power is a means of repression that perpetrates authoritarianism. Authority subdues through power. So authoritarian power is nothing more than the force that deludedly tries to utilize vital energy against life. Authority lacks power, but it utilizes force. Power, on the other hand, can be either authoritarian or liberating.

The structure of power perpetuates authority and irremediably neutralizes, controls, tames and corrupts. Because of this, resistance against power using the same mechanisms as power can be disastrous for resistance movements. This has been the truthful and sad history of the national revolutions of political, social, or economic independence. Authority and power are locked in a vicious circle that snares every attempt to make the passage into open air. Curiously, in the corruption of power and loss of authority lies the force of energy. Corruption of power permits resistance to break the bewildering fence of authority, which is materialized through the arbitrariness of discourse, laws and rules. Its lack of consistency is its weakness. Because of this, in a liberated society the exercise of societal authority should be avoided at all cost. Whichever punishment or sentence culminates in imprisonment and deprivation of liberty of an individual tends to newly construct that authoritarian fence that the standardizing system has perfected through its ultra-sophisticated repressive techniques and from which has originated the present-day panoptic society of control.

In communities—or constellations of peculiarities—dispersed in the open air, power dissipates in force, becoming a means to action and mobility. This is the energy or black matter that, according to quantum physics, does not emit any kind of radiation and is distributed in a similar way to visible material—each one being aware of the presence of the other. Power and authority are worthless in the face of this cosmic energy force. The dilemma consists in not reproducing the dominant logic. Thus, ostracism is a group defense that does not damage the integrity of the free creation of constellations of peculiarities. The decision to expel for a period or permanently—in the case of irresolvable conflicts—a member of the community is much healthier and less threatening to the vital praxis than any other kind of punishment. There is an obvious contrast between ostracism and the aberration of executions—a horrific institutional practice of extermination, genocide and repression.

The means of action and mobility that the energy force is situated in come from the vitality that emanates from the planet and living beings. Their source is the very same nature that maintains all of the creatures that inhabit the

earth-garden. It is, what's more, a magnetic energy, concentrated and indestructible, and it can
dismantle authority and the power structure without major effort. In the same way, thinking of the
system as something powerful is laughable. The
capacity to depose it is in our spirit. And not even
all of its technical apparatus of intimidation, control
and death can stop the avalanche of energizing
force when it erupts. This is the true human
power. It is needless to say that before life on
this planet is extinguished by way of pollution
and the irresponsibility of the present-day self-
destructive model, all human traces—and certainly
civilization itself—will disappear from the face of
the earth. This will happen inexorably if we do
not correct with absolute urgency the sinister
direction assigned by the rudder of standardization. Otherwise, nothing will remain except for a
pair of skulls in whose molars will be found an
herbivorous nature with a carnivorous past.

35

NOT BEING CIVILIZED means being
outside of standardization. For example, to
pronounce a word erroneously according to the
dictionary, in opposition to common sense and the

phonetic rhythm of the language, or to go against the given use of a particular linguistic community is to throw a rock at the tyrannical minute hand of uniformity. Television has been in the last forty years the sinister vehicle of standardization. It has not only imposed a way of speaking, but also of seeing and of dreaming. Uncivilizing oneself means breaking with mediacratic homogeneity. To liberate oneself it is necessary to grasp the uniqueness of each and every one, that which constitutes the innate peculiarity of the being. The poverty of progress is a product of self-standardization. Ideologically, self-standardization means successfully learning the modern training in order to think during the entire course of a life in linear and progressive terms. This vision of time, which determines the modern perception of reality, makes every subject live life according to planned goals and promises that never end up happening. This generates anxiety: the first step toward alienation and toward postmodern emptiness that launches itself into the abyss of nonsense. Another form of self-standardization is to internalize the control of authoritarian power through paranoid and self-repressive behavior. This reinforces self-censorship and denies spontaneity by classifying it as noxious and inconvenient. As compensation, it offers improvisation, which is conduct that does not ponder or weigh the effects of human action on the planet and all other living beings, thus negating the eternal inhalation and exhalation of the rhythm of life. "Savagery" is liberating oneself from the poverty of progress, which is nothing more than the symbiotic mix of "povgress," the registered trademark of the civilizing product, whose postmark and barcode have been stamped in the office of standardization. "Savagery" is, among other things, the only possible richness, because it brims with peace, abounds in time, and has life and spontaneity to spare. "Savagery" enriches the spirit.

36

THE WORLD is the projection of consciousness; a world without consciousness is one-dimensional. The standardizing machine tends to homogenize consciousness in its attempt to wipe it away.

The automaton lacks consciousness because it lacks reality. When all consciousnesses project their peculiarities on reality, the notion and sensation of the world is created. Given that language configures consciousness, consciousness projects itself through language. The importance of language lies in its capacity to construct the world as well as in its talent for verbalizing experience. Thus, it is useless to argue against generative linguistics, which advocates a "deep structure" in all languages in order to prove the existence of an innate mechanism in the human brain that permits each subject to learn languages and create neologisms. Whether or not language is innate has no relevance. What is important is that through language the subject can liberate itself because in this way it is able to verbalize and construct its experience in accordance with its image of the world. This text is proof enough of that. Other texts that will refute it are also proof. The opposite would be muteness, censorship, silencing, persecution and jail, sufficient proof that true language challenges control.

When the standardizing machine enters into action, it imposes a language without sense— the Orwellian newspeak—and an unreal consciousness and world. In this standardized reality, language as well as consciousness and the world seem to be alienating entities and reflections of standardization. This is the trap set by ideology. Its objective is to keep us tense, nervous and insecure, as well as to deny us love and hope. Thus, they will achieve their aim if they keep us mute and incapable of articulating our experience. Self-censorship

and the tangled tongue, which stumbles in its inelo-
quence, both originate in the action of control.

Words can be serious—and also magical—
because they concentrate the energy that permits
the movement of the world, like the wind that
dances in the leaves of the trees. That is art and
poetry—the dance of landscape that lights our
eyes and ourselves when we dance in the foliage.

37

IF IDENTITY separates the subject from other
subjects and nature, consciousness reattaches
it. Clearly, without consciousness, there is no
possible change. Clarity and good sense are acts
of consciousness because they permit a comprehension of existence itself within the frame of the
totality of life. Consciousness feeds the imagination
that operates under creative processes. Intelligence,
on the other hand, proceeds rationally in that it
stores data, processes information, establishes
associations, is self-aware, problematizes and
gives answers. It also adapts, questions and fan-
tasizes. Fantasy is the product of a peculiar kind
of creation: Alice in Wonderland, for example.
Imagination, however, opens the possibilities for
the eternal fan of creation.

Consciousness can also be self-destructive and lead to suicide. The ending of one's life by motu proprio is only possible through an act of consciousness. It is, according to Albert Camus, an act of absolute freedom. This generally occurs when consciousness is paralyzed by the standardizing action that dispels imagination. When consciousness does not imagine—which is, after all, how it expresses itself—it self-destructs. Aesthetic manifestation of the being is impossible when imagination is annuled.

38

TECHNOLOGICAL appliances seem neutral. But in reality they are not because they have a purpose. In effect, if they are used, they make an indelible impact on consciousness. Thus, they also make the user dependent: dominated, cretinized, infantilized, and tied to the stake of alienation. However, if appliances are not used, they deteriorate, rust, are infested with ants, or otherwise simply disappear from consciousness. In a similar sense, all technological artifacts divide humans into users and non-users. Those who advocate their use will not hesitate to use their technological weapons of destruction and war in order to dominate those who have no contact with technology. That is how it has been, and that is how it is now.

Technology also divides through its domesticating effect. People work in order to buy electronic appliances or other articles that promote technology, or simply to have access to the services offered by technology that generally promise entertainment or comfort, as well as increased capacity to perform certain actions (to fly, for example, from one continent to another, to paste documents on a word processor, to use a video camera to record daily events with or to document police brutality in order to denounce it). Technology mediates human relations. It drives to insanity, isolates or connects, giving a common cultural reference to many people who talk, live and communicate by and through technological culture. In this way, reality and the world homogenize themselves in accordance with the different programs of the standardizing agenda. This uniformity is reinforced by the clear-cutting of forests, the construction of malls, racial profiling, and so on and so forth. Technology intervenes in all of these processes, which would not be possible without the accelerated destruction of the environment.

This seems inarguable: technology is an apparatus one uses, throws away, forgets or never has access to. Technology alienates. Technology consumes and mediates human life. But technology is also a form of approximation of reality filtered by a functional mental module that arises in ideology. This is technological reason.

The sieve that separates the subject from its surroundings and bursts the cocoon of consciousness constructs human rationality. The stagnation of reason in its instrumental practices develops the technological filter. And this petrifies consciousness. Consciousness has an immediate effect that affects other consciousnesses, producing a general or social consciousness. In this way, there are no isolated consciousnesses, because when one interacts with another, the consciousness of both is modified, altering, at the same time, global consciousness.

Technological reason has made consciousness begin to standardize itself, standardizing everything simultaneously. In order to self-peculiarize—and also peculiarize everything—and to create a better understanding of totality and the self, it is necessary to steer consciousness toward aesthetic reason. In an aesthetic reality, all the possibilities of the imagination would open, and social consciousness would be created in a way that is distinct from the blind and bewildering way it is stimulated by mass society. This would lead to the reestablishment of social relationships by way of the logical and analogical reasoning that already exists in every peculiarity of nature. In order to do so, it is fundamental that we give loose rein to our being and let it express itself in the perennial present as a simple aesthetic expression. Every peculiarity shines with its own light in its meeting with every other being that connects with all and with life.

39

ALL LIVING CREATURES have an impact on nature, including the plants and trees, which stay silent before the pendular night and day. Ants not only affect nature, they also affect humans. Of the 7,600 classified species, a small number cause an infinity of damage as much by their biting, chewing and invading of human habitat as by their boring into gardens, defoliating trees and plants, wrecking constructions, fabrics, wood, electrical installations, appliances and so on.

Ants enslave other insects and violently attack their enemies. Every anthill functions collectively—the ants work in harmony, feeding the queen ant and defending her against foreign aggression. The bellicosity of ants is the product of a highly sophisticated organizational structure which causes them to go so far as to wage wars against other anthills. In the course of the ants' waging of war, the worker ants clear paths to allow the soldier ants passage, while the soldier ants lift branches and twigs that interrupt the escape or triumphal return with termites or other creatures that the ants store as a food or energy source for the winter (when the ants hibernate). Some species of soldier ants have a superior body size to the rest of the colony, which brings about a clear division of functions and tasks. The caste system is tremendously inflexible and efficiently rigid. There is no mobility. In this way, the hierarchy begins with the ant-mother, whose matriarchy rules over the workers and soldiers. The smallest and most agile ants are normally the workers, and they do most of the work. In general, the workers are atrophied females that on occasion grow larger-than-normal mandibles and also dedicate themselves to the defense of the anthill.

Ants appeared in the Cretaceous period, more or less a hundred million years ago. They inhabit every continent in the most diverse climactic conditions. They are essentially social insects, and they communicate with their fellow ants using pheremones. This form of communication—or information transfer—which functions like language, is carried out through the rubbing of their antennae or the exchange of food or other objects. Touch is very important, given that the eyesight of ants is limited. Their vision doesn't reach more than a few centimeters, but their sense of smell is highly developed. According to entomologists, the vocabulary of ants comprises up to ten or twenty chemical signs (the pheromones). Using these signs, ants are able to distinguish their fellows' castes, give warnings about danger, lead from one place to another, maintain the unity of the colony and recognize enemies, food, or unexpected situations. Many colonies of ants live in nests made of earth or wood. In this way, they protect themselves from their enemies and the inclemencies of the weather. What's more, ants store food and other energy resources, for example other insects that they capture and maintain in captivity.

Thomas Belt studied a type of ant in Nicaragua that completely sacks coffee plantations and orange groves. Other ants ferment leaves and enclose aphids in corrals. This practice is the defining feature of their civilization. According to Belt, "some [ants] are in charge of cutting pieces of leaves with their scissor-shaped, while others on the ground transport the leaf fragments to the ant colony. But these leaf fragments are not food for the ants; rather, they let them rot and ferment to form a fertile base in which they carefully insert pieces of mycelium fibers. In this way they cultivate the mushrooms that feed them. But even more surprising is the case of the so-called rancher ants. They take care of and guard aphid populations so that they reproduce to dizzying rhythms until they entirely cover the plants to which they have affixed themselves. The ants caress and fuss over the aphids and are rewarded with a sweet liquid that is, for the ants, an exquisite delicacy. Sometimes they even construct small corrals in the ant colony where they fatten the aphids and their offspring, which they watch with great care." This practice is very similar to human civilization.

Ants are predatory. Plagues of ants, for example, will attack any living organisms they find in their path. Fire ants attack and kill other insects or small animals and tend to feed on dead animals. There are other ants that are nomads and inhabit the desert. In the forest, species of gardener ants are found. In fact, half of the forests of the American continent have been planted by these ants. They protect certain plants and trees from certain harmful insects and diseases. On the shores of the Amazon river, for example, the so-called hanging gardens suspended in the branches of the trees are nothing more than a natural wonder created entirely by gardener ants, which transport leaves and flowers to the highest branches and trunks to construct their nests. This modification of the landscape undoubtedly has a positive impact on nature.

The domus of the ants is known as the anthill. Hundreds of thousands of ants can live there. However, when two of them meet, they only need to touch their antennae to identify one another. Ants accumulate eggs, which the fertile ants put in a designated place within the anthill. Some worker ants act as nursemaids, feeding larvae that weave a silk covering around themselves in order to become nymphs and end their development in complete immobility. When the nymphs break out of their coccoons, they are already fully formed ants that in a few hours will join the common and social work of the colony. The anthills are made up of tunnels and passages that communicate with one another, indicating an architectural consciousness that recalls human cities. If the anthill is found in arid zones, some ants sacrifice themselves in the wet season, bloating themselves on water. They thus maintain—for months, even up to a year—the water needs of the community. If their companions go in search of water, they themselves gently serve it from mouth-to-mouth.

In a conference that took place in August, 2001 in South Africa, the anthropologist Richard Leakey pointed out that the world is suffering from the loss of anywhere from fifty to a hundred thousand species every year due to human activity, which seriously endangers the equilibrium of the planetary ecosystem. This massive extinction is comparable to that which affected the dinosaurs sixty-five million years ago. Clearly, all living creatures have an impact on nature, but the impact of human civilization on the planet is highly destructive. It is calculated that the weight of the ants on the planet equals the weight of the six billion humans who also inhabit the earth. But the impact of human civilization is radically distinct from the effect that ants produce. As a matter of fact, if human beings disappeared from the planet at this moment, it is likely that the ants and many other species that are wiped out every year would survive. On the other hand, if ants disappeared, life on earth would not be possible. The activity of ants is essential for the health of the planet. They not only work and aerate the soil, they also move it and fertilize it, playing an even more important role than earthworms. Ants can move up to twenty tons of soil during the entire lifespan of a colony. In contrast, the insane, destructive and contaminating effects of a single city in its total lifespan are still immeasureable.

40

TERMITES—also known as white ants—are the mortal enemies of ants. Ants capture them and maintain a war to the death against them. Both species compete for the same vital space. Termites gnaw wood and other organic material. Ants can be carnivorous and will even eat others of their kind if the need arises. During the summer, ants store grains and seed as winter provisions.

Termites descend from a family distinct from that of the ants (termites are distant relatives of the cockroach), but they have a system of social organization that is very similar to that of their enemies. Both species build nests to inhabit and develop modes of social life, modifying nature. Some species of ants build their nests in tree trunks, others by gathering and folding leaves to live inside. The majority of ants excavate the soil to form galleries and rooms that are perfectly organized. This is the modified land where they raise their civilization. Termites also construct their colonies—which are similar to isotopic domi—in rafters or the soil. Termite colonies in the soil are hillocks that can reach great heights and take forms that stimulate the imagination. In fact, termite colonies seem artificial designs that make one realize that the best landscape art is found in nature itself. It is only necessary to learn to look. This erases the dividing line between the world and art, a line created early on by ideological instrumentalization and its taxonomic methodologies. Nature is aesthetic in itself.

41

LET'S SPECULATE for a moment. In addition to the current hypothesis about the extinction of the Neanderthals as a lineage separate from the Sapiens about thirty thousand years ago, there are two other hypotheses. One of them argues that in reality there was a process of mixed breeding between the Neanderthals and the Sapiens, which would have meant a gradual disappearance of the Neanderthals due to a slow hybridism hegemonized by the Sapiens. The other hypothesis, a little less optimistic, argues that the Neanderthals disappeared when they were denied access to their traditional hunting and gathering territories by human beings. It is possible that both hypotheses are correct. In this day and age it is almost impossible to sustain positions of racial or evolutionary purity of the humanoid specimens that once inhabited the planet and that, it seems, appeared with Australopithecus, who appeared five million years ago in Africa. It is logical to think then that human beings are completely intermixed.

The face of a Neanderthal child, re-created as a computer model by the paleo-anthropologists Marcia Ponce de León and Christoph Zollikofer at the University of Zurich, illuminates some facts about this humanoid species that it is supposed to have inhabited Northern Europe, the Near East, Central Asia, and, in all likelihood, Western Siberia. The jaws of the Neanderthals—which had almost no chin and strong teeth and molars, well equipped to rip meat and grind roots— demonstrate that the diet of these humanoids was carnivorous. It is likely that, due to their maxillofacial characteristics, they did not have a rich verbal language, but they did have other ways of communicating as well as spiritual and artistic rituals. In contrast with the ants and ter-mites, which maintain an implacable war, or other belligerent species like blowflies, which neglect sucking the nectar of flowers and pollinating in favor of attacking bees and eating flowers, it is very possible that in effect there was a sort of hybridism between Sapiens and Neanderthals. It is also possible that this first mixing provoked a genetic transformation that created a new group of hybrid beings that not only adopted the carnivorous diet as a form of subsistence, but also played a crucial role in the shift toward agriculture. We know that this meant sedentarism and domestication, processes that later devolved into all of the homogenizing forms of organization of collective life. And while human beings are social beings, we also need solitude and leisure.

In contrast with ants and termites, the human world is not constructed only in relation to work. Neither do we spend all of our time in search of food. Instead, sometimes we rest, laugh, or play. We need fun, time off, and idleness. In the hymenoptera world, by contrast, the rigid caste system makes sure that each active member of the colony is always performing its task: the queen-mother (like the machine-mother), the workers, the soldiers and the slaves. This ultra-hierarchical system of social organization is completely lacking in imagination. And the inflexible and efficient societies of standardization approximate it, making sure every member's assigned labor maintains the life of the tremendous and incomprehensible gears. There the machine-mother incubates her eggs and the system is perpetuated. For this reason, slogans like "Imagination to power," "Imagine the impossible," or the Einsteinian maxim, "Imagination is more important than knowledge," keep their validity even while ideological repression and the control panel continue dominating the human race. Although, clearly, this is pure speculation.

42

THE BOURGEOIS garden expanded like a plague under colonialism. It's pretty, but fake. The scenarios installed by civilization, as artistic as they are, lack reality. They require space and the eradication of undesireable species, turning the living world into a backdrop over which the garden can be imposed instantly, like a Polaroid.

The civilizing garden enslaves, torments, and sooner or later, will die. This happens because the bourgeois garden standardizes the land, instead of unfolding it in order to have an open and horizontal space. What's more, its objective is luxury, neglecting the comestible and self-sustainable garden.

The bourgeois garden is about enclosure. In addition, through the illusion of illuminating civilized space, it kills the night. The garden of peculiarities deterritorializes and topples hierarchies.

That is its nature. It allows the garden to grow, organically, under the concept of mutual recognition between the gardener and garden. It doesn't try to control the landscape by making it uniform. On the contrary, the point is learning to live with nature and in the midst of nature, orienting the human effect more toward aesthetic practice than standardization. Such a lesson starts by recognizing the otherness of nature as our own otherness. Only in this way is it possible to dissipate the ego among the ever-growing foliage in search of shelter rather than conquest.

43

THE NOTION of peculiarity opposes standardization and dualism. Standardization flattens and erases biodiversity. In the words of César Vallejo, it is "Lomismo [sameness] that suffers name." Dualism in its own right has sustained the genealogy of cognitive thinking that has constructed disciplines and methodologies through the opposition of terms that are apparently contradictory or equidistantly opposed from one another: A or B, good or bad, light or dark, concrete or abstract, general or particular, bourgeois or proletariat, barbarian or civilized, etc. Indeed, the role of dualism is to simplify, although none of its oppositions can be considered completely true since they are mere, abstract representations of bits of reality and of nature. In the same way, there are no oppositions more radical than others, or less radical, given that the rational procedure itself is an error from the beginning. What do exist are oppositions that are clearer than others because they help us to fully comprehend certain relatively complex processes.

According to the above and following the Lacanian dualist model, which opposes the imaginary with the symbolic, that is to say, the non-structured world of a child who projects images over reality—which is a liberated universe that still hasn't been structured by the formal process of repression of symbols—it is possible to distinguish the following path. Symbols follow from the symbolic, whose orbit includes the civilized order—the patriarchal grammar imposed by society. Following this parallel, images derive from the imaginary, the projection of interiority onto the world. So, images lead to imagination, and symbols lead to symbolization, which in turn manifests itself in rites. The ritual instrumentalizes nature, in order to dominate it via the medium of magic or representation. This instrumentality is functional and coercive because it structures and manipulates. In effect, the different instruments of the symbolic tend to represent reality rather than allow it to be fully comprehended. Images, on the other hand, create the perceptions of the world that are expressed culturally through the aesthetic and underlie culture. When this occurs, the being is manifested aesthetically and unfurls all of its peculiarities. However, instrumentalization brings about standardization, which hides in its innards a controlling beat that categorizes everything through the varied methodologies of taxonomic classification. This process of standardization produces fetish, which is nothing more than a false consciousness of reality. This foundation of false consciousness is the spectacularization of life as well as alienation.

There are two distinct types of insanity. One is material and reduces life to economic survival. The other is ideological and generates dehumanization and roboticization in the subject. Under the spell of automatism, the human being separates him/herself from nature and from his/her own natural condition. With peculiarity, consciousness is created, comprehensively rehumanizing and reconnecting human beings with themselves and with nature. Consciousness is neither intelligence nor knowledge. It is the recognition of the other, and the recognition that the relationship to the other does not exist solely in exclusive, Hegelian, dialectic terms of the master and slave. Recognition can also be inclusive. Consciousness allows coexistence based on mutual respect and reciprocal recognition of others, who are nothing less than our counterparts: the environment and creatures that inhabit it and that constitute totality. Coexistence is only possible through a corresponding comprehension of the peculiarity of all beings in order to establish a radical empathy for the right of all beings to life.

44

THE IMAGE that our interiority projects on the world maintains its aesthetic character. The image that has been reflected reinforces the process of reification. In and of themselves, all images that separate us alienate us. Each image is an act of reification, given that these images represent reality, establishing mediation among human beings and between the subject and the natural surroundings. This mediation replaces reality. When the prehistoric child saw its own face in the water's reflection—in a lake, a pool or the ice—it saw nothing but an image. This equation led it to identify itself with what it was seeing, thus awakening the notion of identity. This notion led to the separation between the individual and nature and fed the fracture between the subject and the object—the foundation of human consciousness. In this way, consciousness gives rise to alienation, and becomes meta-consciousness: self-reflection on itself. However, without self-reflective consciousness, the human being is defenseless against the imperial control of standardization and the propaganda machine that falsifies reality and manufactures a false and ideological consciousness.

Modern industrial alienation works by denying the present and forcing the subject to live in a kind of virtual reality that goes by the name of "future." The modern mentality is characterized by planning for the future. This notion pierces the human mind like a steel bar running through a line of individuals working on the assembly line. The horizon of the future is experienced as unlimited time that advances progressively in a blind race with no meaning or end. For the premodern, religious mentality, the future is finite and ends in the final judgment or the ascension of the believer to whatever paradise happens to be promoted by a particular mythical-religious narrative. In this way, both the modern and the premodern fix a temporality that is outside of the perpetual present, thus inscribing the human mentality in the camp of domestication. Experiencing the present, in the here and now, leads to a predomestic state and rebels against the ideas of planning and development. The notion of the future is therefore an image that reflects ideology. And it's no mystery to anyone that the fruition of the future inhabits the arena of the impossible although its arrival may be inevitable.

.45

DIFFERENCE homogenizes and makes uniform experience in two blocks that are supposedly different. This is part of dualism. Beta is different from alpha and vice-versa. In accordance with this binomial practice, difference determines identity. But this is the trap of categorization, a strategy of the standardizing empire. Understanding identity in this way is to conceive it in belligerent, antagonistic and opposing terms. Thus the peculiarity of each being is denied. Each creature is peculiar and different from all other creatures, who are peculiar and different among themselves. Difference reduces identity to only two identifying blocks: alpha or beta, gamma or epsilon or any other pair. The peculiarity of the self unties binary binds and amplifies our self-reflective consciousness, the bridge necessary for comprehending the experience of the being in totality. This comprehension necessarily requires a "new humanity." This is the "new world" that we construct every time we disconnect from the standardizing machines and live our lives in a different way and more naturally in order to de-alienate ourselves and cure ourselves from the sickness of ideology, injected by the syringe of propaganda. And difference is one more trap of propaganda.

46

BARBARA EHRENREICH proposes that wars, like ritual sacrifice, are celebratory practices that reconstruct the transition of the human animal from prey to predator. It may be that human violence is the residual memory of the repressed experience of having been prey, our original place in the food chain. Through socialization and cooperation, primitive bands were able to survive the attacks of predators. Notwithstanding, the weakest, slowest, and defenseless were given up for the good of the entire primitive clan. As soon as the youngest and healthiest members were able to flee, the beasts had a feast, devouring those left behind. This awoke a sense of danger and terror that engendered the consciousness of death. Sociability was a first step toward survival, giving rise to feelings of solidarity and community cooperation. The experience of being prey is before that of being hunter. It was only the manufacture of tools and their manipulation that permitted humans to hunt other animals for food and in self-defense. In this way they also sharpened domesticating practices. The dog, for example, was mastered primarily as an animal for the hunt. It is probable, however, that humans first engaged in scavenging, which gave rise to carnivorous practice. With the working and polishing of stone—the fabrication of tools and weapons for hunting—human beings derailed the course of nature and converted themselves into predators. This originated bellicose thinking, and at the same time lay the foundation of the instrumental, evolving development of reasoning. In this process, carnivorous animals were viewed as deities, represented many times in prehistoric cave paintings and symbolic rites. This representation is tied to the practice of sacrifice, which, for example, the ancient Greeks transformed into hecatombs. Wars are nothing more than bellicose rites of human sacrifice carried out in the name of "political fathers" who have designed the standardizing and stupefying megamachine. Wars re-enact the horror of being prey and stimulate the adrenaline rush of fight or flight; meanwhile, they also heighten the conquering spirit of the predator. In modern societies, antidepressants have suppressed adrenaline, repressing the capacity to experience risk and subsuming instinct in self-repressive and stressful frustration. The megamachine cretinizes the population, which becomes a group of superfluous individuals easily manipulated by nationalistic slogans, derived perhaps from a socializing and pristine original sentiment. Militarism drives soldiers to a modern hecatomb, whose only effect is terror. In the face of this terror, climbing trees to defend them from clearcutting, liberating animals from their cages, letting deer graze peacefully, organizing communal meals, hugging friends, etc., are acts of love that thwart the logic of the hunted and hunter. War is the material and symbolic re-enactment of the transition to predation, and it crystallizes in the "terrorist" reliving of horror. The utmost respect for all living creatures is the only possible ethic that can oppose depredating aggression. Survival is not sustained in the art of killing, or in politics, or in war. On the contrary, responsible cooperation and community are essential for human and planetary coexistence. Predation, terror and war are the sanguine trident of instrumental reason, and its self-rationalizing logic is the foolishness that annihilates consciousness and steeps the imagination in fear. In order to amplify the consciousness to the detriment of genetic determinism, it is necessary to banish the paradigm of prey-predator. Opposing war is a first step.

47

A CCORDING to anarcho-primitivist thought, the division of labor produced a reifying sequence that led to the construction of the symbolic with all its ramifications: numeration, art, technology, agriculture, language, culture, etc. Therefore, the symbol is the dividing line between prehistoric life, full of sensual vitality, and current historical life, mediated by reification and delirious with alienation. According to Marxism, this division was produced when society was stratified into classes that were cemented by the appropriation of land and knowledge by a group of priests who unfurled the map of social petrification into dominant and dominated classes: masters and slaves, feudal lords and serfs, bourgeois and proletariat, etc. In either interpretation, it is recognized that there was a fracture between prehistoric and historic time: feral primitivism in contrast to civilization and domestication, or primitive communism as opposed to the society of classes and social exploitation. The precise dating of this rupture varies according to the anthropological source consulted as well as the perspectives of the different agendas subscribed to by believers in "science," but it is generally agreed that the adoption of agriculture was the crucial moment in the great turn toward sedentary, hierarchical, and repressive life. Notwithstanding, and in spite of the established consensus, it is much more probable that the "expulsion" from the primitive paradise dates back to an earlier moment than the data usually support. It was that moment when we human beings began to distinguish ourselves from nature: the point when consciousness, identity and language formed the triangle that simultaneously severed us from the natural world and created the notion of humanity.

Human consciousness arises precisely from its separation from the larger consciousness of nature and the cosmos, to which animals, insects, vegetables, are still connected. Our consciousness separates us from nature, producing an unavoidable division. It arises from two processes that have to do with identification and verbalization. The first refers to the notion of identity produced by the recognition of one's own death. Consciousness of one's own mortality generates the idea of an "I" formed in opposition to the identity of the other: everyone else, nature, the animal world, etc. This basic opposition between interiority and exteriority is made understandable through verbalization. The subject enunciates—mentally or phonetically—the signified "I", and it leads to the notion of the external and the other—I am what the other is not. This initiates early on subjection to a table of contents and arbitrary signs that are represented a posteriori in the form of a grammar and that tend to reveal the sense of an "I" and a "non-I," the psychological basis of the projection of self over nature. Such a process of self-comprehension of identity through language leads to the animist experience of nature. Therefore, a spirit or "anima," which inhabits all the elements in the world, can be perceived. It is likely that at this moment humans were herbivorous gatherers whose slowly developing processes of identification and verbalization caused them to initiate cannibalistic practices, as a ritual ratification of their collective identities, which were later transformed into carnivorism. This is the age of hunting, fishing and gathering—besides the change in our position on the food chain.

The rite leads to the symbolic because through it the impulse to dominate the "powers" of nature arises. This happens through the ceremonial practices that are coded in symbolic acts with a ritualistic origin. In the symbol is found the germ of all reifying practices that derive from the divorce between the appreciation of nature and practical coexistence within nature. This separation fosters the instrumentalization of the environment whose first manifestation is found in the shamanic magic that aspires to modify nature through supernatural power. Shamanism is the practice of the invocation of the spirit of the elements—perceived in the animist phase—so as to order the course of nature according to the will of the shaman or witch. Thus symbolic instrumentality represents the material world of nature, which, little by little, is replaced by the symbol itself.

The Neanderthals developed figures and hunting and musical instruments thirty thousand years ago, at the very least. And certain Australian aboriginal groups developed symbolic ornaments more than fifty thousand years ago. This mediation by symbolic instruments modified thinking and imposed a rational, logical and functional mental module that expanded unchecked over the intuitive and the aesthetic. This instrumental reason generated technological thinking, which led to categorization, the base of all standardizing practice. Thus, the division of labor became more complex, giving origin to class societies and civilization: history. Art, the state, language, economy, money, races, technology, colonization, etc. are embedded there. Likewise, domestication also began its ultimate realization in history, as much through agriculture and symbolic culture as through ranching and the norming of wilderness, which leads to clearcutting. Modern profit and alienation are forms of social domestication on a massive scale through the expansion of the production line. The instrumental therefore is the source of all hierarchical and categorical entities, which are nothing more in themselves than a set of ideas about reality accumulated over time. These are the ideas that consitute the ideology of progress and history. Indeed, this ideology has fed the empire of standardization and dualistic thinking.

The notion of the peculiar radically dismantles dualism and standardization in that it allows the human being to reconnect with the natural world through appreciation of and aesthetic interaction with nature. This not only debunks the false division between art and reality that uproots all beauty from life, it also destroys instrumental reason, which gives origin to all alienating notions that perpetuate the symbolic. The appreciation of nature implies also its defense in the course of an active practice of organic coexistence. This includes a total respect for all the living creatures of the planet and a social cohabitation that guarantees the ritual retribution of every primal material extracted from the land and the forest.

Beginning today to cultivate one's own sustenance in organic gardens that respect the ecosystem is a vital necessity. Community life guarantees independence and autonomy from the corporate and state system. Community life values personal relationships without hierarchical or bureaucratic mediation and stimulates camaraderie and brother and sisterhood based on the principle of cooperation. Realizations of this have been achieved in different communities around the globe, such as Christiania (Denmark), Aprovecho and Alpha Farm (both in Oregon, USA), Solentiname (Nicaragua), Gaviotas (Colombia), GAIA (Costa Rica), etc. In North America alone there are around four thousand community experiments, without counting the ancestral indigenous communities throughout the Americas that continue to resist western colonizing penetration.

The general solution with respect to industrial agriculture and monoculture is permaculture, which does not squander natural resources and permits sustainable ways of life in harmony with the environment and its diverse microclimates. The planet is a constellation of microclimates or meteorological peculiarities where the flowering of rotating and mobile human communities is possible. The notion of an ideal and exclusive climate for survival is a sophism of standardization. Just as humans are a peculiar genus of nature, so are climates, valleys, mountains, coasts, forests, plains, etc. To feel in order to understand is a tactic of self-sensitivization. Sensitivity reconnects us to the earth and makes us wise. To live in a community implies living in harmony with the soil on which we tread, the air we breathe, the breeze that washes us, the forest that feeds us, the water that gives us life, etc. To live in community is to live with others. But it is also living inside an environment and climate that are peculiar. To feel this peculiarity is to guarantee survival.

Sabotage against the infantilizing machine and against the agro-industrial complex—which profits at the expense of the health of the soil and people—has also been a tactic of present day self-defense in some communities on the planet.

Resistance against the penetration of timber companies and against the construction of hydroelectric dams has been the catalyst for a new biocentric consciousness. Take for example the cases of Mapuche communities in southern Chile and green activists in the Pacific Northwest who literally take to the trees—constructing platforms within the tree canopy itself to block clear cutting in old-growth forests. These examples of integrity wake the sleeping consciousness suppressed by the empire of standardization. When such consciousness flowers, it opposes the monetarist agenda of the oligopolies, thus reestablishing the imagination and opening the gates to a new world.

The creative consciousness of the twenty-first century began to express itself in 1999 with the student strike at the National Autonomous University in Mexico City and the struggle in Seattle against the World Trade Organization. In that same year, on the 18th of June, an anarchist protest occurred in Eugene, Oregon. Meanwhile, peasant actions, notably the attack in the south of France on a fast-food restaurant and another against transnational sites producing genetically modified food in Brazil, awakened the ecosocial creative consciousness to a greater range of concerns. This has generated a resistance movement that has grown organically at every protest against so-called globalization, obliging corporate agents to barricade themselves inside the protective fences erected and guarded by the praetorian battalions of the standardizing empire. This happened in Prague, in Quebec, and in Genoa, and it will continue to happen. It is precisely this walling in that isolates the system and is causing it to topple under its own weight, leading toward self-demolition. Thus, the destruction on September 11, 2001 of the pillars of global capitalism, symbolized by the number eleven that formed the twin towers of the World Trade Center in New York, has opened an irreparable tear in the plastic bubble of the empire of standardization. This is the beginning of the end and inaugurates a new era in the quest for the ancestral wisdom found in the garden of each and every peculiarity.

When Columbus arrived on the "American" continent, the European colonizing enterprise began its march, and with it, standardization. In five hundred years, 75% of the native comestible plants of the Americas have disappeared—among them many legumes with proteins similar to soy. As an extension of the invaders' genocide, many European plants were transported to the continent, invading the soil and destroying the biodiversity of the native ecosystems. In truth, rational European knowledge was much more limited than the ancestral knowledge of the native communities of the continent, who understood much better natural cycles. In the fifteenth century, Europeans knew only seventeen varieties of edible vegetables, while in the fourth century, the Hohokam—inhabitants of the region now encompassed by New Mexico, cultivated around two hundred varieties of vegetables. In South America, the Incas designed a system of terrace cultivation that extended the length of the Andes and took advantage of local microclimates and varying humus qualities, harvesting something like six hundred different varieties of potatoes. This proves that horticulture has nothing to do with the standardizing drive of civilization. Instead of trying to make all environments conform to a standard medium, horticulture seeks to adapt to the peculiar characteristics of the soil and microclimate while maintaining intact the ecosystem and biodiversity.

The aesthetic peculiarities of different kinds of resistance—each peculiar in and of itself—have uplifted the centuries-long battles of indigenous communities, whose most eloquent forms of self-defense have been manifested in the state of Chiapas (southern Mexico), in Araucanía—Mapuche territory (southern Chile), in Salta (northern Argentina), as well as Bolivia, Ecuador, Colombia and so on. The consciousness of the human species awakens and begins to shake off instrumental reason, all the while finding a path toward the world of peculiarity, toward the natural world itself. In contrast with the primitive consciousness that provoked this fragmentation in the first place, present collective consciousness searches for connection with the other by dispelling the ego in the organic totality of the planet. The dilution of the "I" in the spirit of nature allows the being to fully manifest itself. This manifestation is the aesthetic expression of peculiarity and through it is created a culture that undoes standardization and tears away all of the labels made by the system of categorization. Indeed, when the being unfolds all the petals of its peculiarity to express itself aesthetically, it is able to better itself as well as the world and humanitiy. This process nears authenticity—the condition of the "genuine" that in highly alienated and alienating societies is a privilege almost entirely exclusive to artists and other personalities of exception. In the same way, creative verbalization subverts dualism and reconstructs the notion of humanity. And this is why real conversation is not welcome in the robotic world of the postmodern paradigm of automatons. Hence, expressions like "feral" in English and "bárbaro" in Spanish have started to acquire positive connotations that dismember, via language, the patriarchical model based on the dualistic system of savagery versus civilization.

To think of a remodeled world that permits coexistence based on total and mutual respect for all the creatures that inhabit the planet is vital. Each peculiarity is a petal that is necessary to care for. A horizontal and nonhierarchical model is crucial, since no one likes to be ordered, controlled, or detained. On the contrary, these situations appear to be a punishment. True liberty depends on the demolition of all authority. The natural state of human beings is anarchy, which is nothing more than an ample libertarian garden where the spirit expresses itself. Against the control panel of the standardizing empire, the garden of peculiarities stands healthy. And given that in the earth resides true power, the challenge of this century is a return to daily interaction with nature to heal from the trauma of civilization. That is, to remodel ourselves toward the betterment of our human condition. Only by constructing a new humanity will it be possible to inhabit a new world, based on aesthetic reasoning and sensitivity. And while this is only a point of departure, the rest remains a mystery. There is no panacea for the future.

Just as in the last hundred years the global population has exploded at a frightening rate, it can also decrease in a hundred years. A sensible relationship with the earth that establishes the lost coherence between our reproductive tendencies and the availability of local resources can greatly reduce the number of human beings on the planet. And that can be done without bloodthirsty plans. To know where we are, how we live and how we survive will expand the global consciousness. In addition, it makes us active and responsible participants in the process of human continuity, returning to the people their ancestral independence—freedom from both mass production and industrial medicine. Toward the beginning and middle of the twentieth century, couples generally had five or more children. In colonized countries, and especially in the countryside and in other entirely dispossessed zones, this tendency continues as a strategy for survival. When clothing, food, and shelter are wrested from the monopoly control of commercial chains and mass production and are returned to the hands of the community, community responsibility and autonomy will transform

140

human consciousness into an integral consciousness, thus reuniting the being with the community
and the environment. And this will transform
present day reproductive tendencies. And it will
ensure that in one or two generations overpop-
ulation will be nothing more than a "problem"
from the industrial past.

The garden of peculiarities is a project of
humanity. Its visualization consists of realizing
the peculiarity of nature. If the original consciousness grew as a result of the recognition of
its own death, liberating consciousness will grow
as a result of the recognition of its own peculiarity. Life as we conceive of it today will not be
erased from the planet as long as we don't give
respite to the empire of "sameness." The point is
to learn to live in the planetary garden without
control or authority. And if life is a voyage, it is
necessary to let ourselves be carried along with
the river's current without imposing a control to
stop it. The current of the river is the current of
nature. The social current, standardizing and
"medio-cratic," is the electricity of control. To
continue in this vein is to die of stress, alienation,
anxiety, insanity, hunger, exploitation, repression, and misery. In order to run the rapids it is
necessary to learn to live. When one follows the
silvery movement of each tumultuous and savage

drop of water, one is creating contact with the rhythm of the natural world. To follow this cadence, avoiding the rocks is a wise act. To fall from the raft is evidence of discomfort. This discomfort is the incompatibility between control and life. Control engenders fear and impedes life. It unleashes paranoia. Life, on the other hand, offers beauty and ingenuity as its native fruits. It depends on us to bite the apple and to learn to dream.

The voyage to the garden of peculiarities is one without return. To listen to the murmuring of civilization, once on the correct path, is to fall into the trap of fear. It means losing one's way, because the only exit is the escape hatch to the highway that leads to the asphalt of standardization. And while every creature needs a dwelling, it need not be made of concrete. The true human lair can be a cabin in the forest that together with other cabins forms a community of peculiarities. Or it can be a neighborhood that tears up the pavement of idiocy and isolation while leaving one or two routes among other neighborhoods. Each constellation of peculiarities will be a kind of commune that guarantees the horizontal autonomy of each community. Only in this way can hierarchy be abolished. And as social practice between social beings, ritual festivities and community celebration will be an integral part of the strategy to combat accumulation. In this way, all surplus that will eventually be created will be enjoyed as a part of the collective carnival.

The garden of peculiarities is a wager made for the conservation of the environment and the survival of the human race. There intuition should light the way. Not being sidetracked depends on us. There is only one path that leads to the heart of life.

ALSO FROM FERAL HOUSE

AGAINST CIVILIZATION
READINGS AND REFLECTIONS
Edited by John Zerzan

Feral House's new expanded edition of *Against Civilization* adds 18 new essays and feral illustrations by R.L. Tubbesing to the contemporary classic that provides 67 thought-provoking looks into the dehumanizing core of modern civilization, and the ideas that have given rise to the anarcho-primitivist movement. The editor of this compelling anthology is John Zerzan, author of *Running on Emptiness* and *Future Primitive.*

6 x 9 • 276 pages • illustrated • $14.00 • ISBN: 0-922915-98-9

WAR IS A RACKET
THE ANTIWAR CLASSIC BY AMERICA'S MOST DECORATED GENERAL
By General Smedley D. Butler • Introduction by Adam Parfrey

General Butler's notorious 1933 speech, "War is a Racket," excoriates "the small inside group" that "knows what the racket is all about." The Feral House edition provides more rare anti-imperialist screeds and an exposé of a Congressional inquiry into Butler's whistleblowing of a coup d'état attempt by big business against Franklin Delano Roosevelt.

5 x 8 • 84 pages • paperback original • ISBN: 0-922915-86-5 • $9.95

RUNNING ON EMPTINESS
THE PATHOLOGY OF CIVILIZATION
By John Zerzan

"Today's pundits are quick to assume the contrarian mantle, but John Zerzan does the hard work to earn it. He runs deeply against the tide familiar arguments from the left and right. Pay attention to his wake— you'll find your definition of 'liberty' suddenly expanding."
—James MacKinnon, senior editor, *Adbusters*

5 1/2 x 8 1/2 • paperback original • 214 pages • ISBN: 0-922915-75-X • $12.00

TO ORDER FROM FERAL HOUSE:
Individuals: Send check or money order to Feral House, P.O. Box 39910, Los Angeles CA 90039, US For credit card orders: call (800) 967-7885 or fax your info to (323) 666-3330. CA residents please add 8.25% sales tax. U.S. shipping: add $4.50 for first item, $2 each additional item. Shipping to Canada and Mexico: add $9 for first item, $6 each additional item. Other countries: add $11 for first item, $9 each additional item. Non-U.S. originated orders must include international money order or check for U funds drawn on a U.S. bank. We are sorry, but we cannot process non-U.S. credit cards.
www.feralhouse.com